FreedomPOINT

PRAISE FOR FREEDOMPOINT

"Deb Battersby's understanding of the role of emotion to all of life and success-building is rare and unique. Further to this, she holds uncommonly high standards when it comes to transforming emotional patterns and unconsciously held traits, understanding that no one need settle for the less-than-ideal experiences they've been subject to until now. In this work she generously hands over the practical applications of her wisdom so that everyone might partake in vastly more nuanced, freeing and powerful emotional experiences in this lifetime. This is a book that delivers."

— Judymay Murphy, International Speaker and Success Coach

"As a client and a certified FreedomPOINT practitioner, I have witnessed how Deb's method helps people let go of inner resistance to hundreds of emotional patterns that are causing blockages in their lives. This method quickly and effectively helps individuals transcend their disempowering beliefs and achieve new levels of wellbeing."

— Catalina D. Fiore, E.M.B.A., MSc, Accredited Master Coach

"Deb's FreedomPOINT method enabled me to elevate my life in extraordinary ways I never imagined were possible. I have more courage, confidence, focus, determination, and creativity in my daily life. I highly recommend Deb to anyone who wants to discover the patterns that are holding them back from transforming and evolving into their best self."

— Dr. Josefina Miranda

"In my 27+ years of experience as an executive coach and a teacher of top executive coaches, Deb Battersby stands out for her style, depth, impact, professionalism, and most of all, her results. Her skillful, elegant, and powerful approach is amazing for its speed and effectiveness at getting to the root of issues, obstacles, and blocks—and moving her clients to their higher ground of capability and performance. A joy to work with, Deb is clearly one of the best of the best. I highly recommend her as a world-class coach and trainer you should get to know."

— Steve Lishansky, Hall of Fame Executive Coach,
CIO Strategic Leadership Mentor & Advisor,
Author of *The Ultimate Sales Revolution*

"Deb is the best strategist coach I have ever worked with in my career. I have been blessed to be working with her for a decade. Her ability to get right to the point and move through any situation with ease and grace is amazing. When I was looking to open a new business, within a few hours, Deb removed all the blocks that were getting in my way, and I built a million-dollar business. Today I am more fulfilled than I have ever been. She has been a gift to me."

— Lisa Lieberman-Wang, Business and Life Strategist,
FINE to FAB

"Reading Deb's book was like taking a journey to my own emotional center. I felt the power of her work in her words as I was reading them. Throughout the book, I went through a range of emotions: hopeful, calm, excited, disappointed, relieved, and by the end, definitely free. The metaphors Deb uses to teach the concepts makes them very easy to understand and, therefore, easy to apply immediately. I'm grateful Deb has written this book and shared her FreedomPOINT method with all of us. It will make the world an even better place."

— Lorraine Tegeris, Personal Development Consultant

"The FreedomPOINT Certification gave me the necessary tools to elevate my private practice's services, equipping me to guide clients to release any unwanted emotional pattern, limiting belief, or thoughts that have been holding them back from experiencing healthy, loving, and passionate relationships. I highly recommend the FreedomPOINT method to any professional to help guide clients to break through any limitations so they can unleash their true essence."

— Bianca Veloso White, Relationship Coach,
Founder of Brave Hearts Coaching

"The FreedomPOINT method is brilliant — exquisitely loving, attuned to leverage points in the subconscious so you can truly rewire the old patterns and beliefs that undermine you. With Deb or one of her trained practitioners, do it! A FreedomPOINT session grants immediate freedom."

— Jim Treadway, Founder, Growth Wise,
Certified FreedomPOINT Practitioner

"I had the privilege to witness and observe Deb helping individuals and groups to move from pain to freedom. Her unique P.O.I.N.T. method sounds a bit like witchcraft, but it truly is magic. Personally, she worked her magic for and with me, transforming my victimhood, which resulted from my brother's suicide, into a story of freedom and glory that laid the foundation for me get my degree as a psychotherapist. One of the funniest, most intelligent, and in-depth people I know, Deb sees beyond the masks and sees the reality. She is always full of love and willing to accompany others through their pain with a "whatever it takes" attitude."

— Doris Möhsl, Psychotherapist, Coach, and Human Being

"If you want to experience a profound yet gentle process that can take the emotional patterns that have been holding you back your entire life and dissolve them instantly, I highly recommend you call Deb Battersby NOW!"

— Courtney Monson

"I've worked with several mindset coaching and personal mentors over the years and my session with Deb brought one of the biggest breakthroughs I've ever had. Deb helped me recognize that where I thought I was craving the emotion of "comfort," what I was really craving was "nurture." With Deb's help, my subconscious identified and intensified where I need to plug into nurture in my life."

— Amy Walker, Amy Walker Consulting

"As owner of a $70 million company with over 300 employees, I was under intense pressure when I first hired Deb as my coach. I got spectacular results in my personal life and my business. Massively reducing stress and commensurately increasing my resourcefulness, I became more effective than ever before. A year later I brought Deb in as a business consultant to work with our leadership team on key initiatives, and the results have far exceeded my expectations. We are set to grow the company and its profits by more than double over the next few years."

— Mark Hunter, CEO Hunter Express

"Deb was so spot on; I was truly impressed by what happened in our sessions. She helped our team identify our roadblocks and areas for immediate growth. I felt very comfortable with her."

— Jasmin Romic, Managing Director of Quiddity

"This was such a powerful process for identifying and uncovering all the emotions that were holding me back and seeing how those emotions may have served me. I had carried emotions around for so long and they needed to go. Deb took me through the process of what the emotions were, where they were located in my body, and what needed to happen to transform them or get rid of them completely. At the end of the process, I had this amazing feeling of joyful lightness. It was really powerful and transforming."

— Beth Assaf

"For the past 17 years, Deb has been a guardian of my subconscious, protector of my heart, and an angel in my life. Her groundbreaking method has been transformative beyond my wildest imagination. She has brought light when there has been darkness. I am infinitely grateful that she is in my life and honored to be in hers."

— Chaniel Cooper

"Working with Deb has been life changing. Her FreedomPOINT method is by far the best experience in personal coaching/personal growth I have had. Deb has been able to pinpoint and release underlying emotional patterns and behaviors I didn't even realize were there. The transformation I have experienced is astonishing! My only regret is not working with her sooner. I tell all my friends, 'Deb is the human ayahuasca!'"

— Rolf Magener

FreedomPOINT

HEAL YOUR HEART,
LIVE YOUR POTENTIAL,
TRANSFORM YOUR LIFE

DEBORAH BATTERSBY

Co-written with and composed
by International Best-Selling Litterateur,

CHRIS DRABENSTOTT

ARCANE
PUBLISHING
Arcane Publishing, LLC
Los Angeles, CA

FreedomPOINT

Arcane Publishing, LLC
Los Angeles, CA

First printing, March 2022

ISBN: 978-1-7348638-3-3 (Paperback)
ISBN: 978-1-7348638-4-0 (eBook)

Published in the United States of America

Deborah A. Battersby, Author
Chris Drabenstott, Co-Writer
Mark Hunter, Writer of Foreword

Book design by Chris Drabenstott, Arcane Publishing, LLC
Cover design by Goldin Productions
Edited by Catherine Black

This book is written as a practical guide to understanding your emotions, the intention behind them, and how you can achieve liberation when accessing them for information and guidance. The concepts, examples, and stories in this book are provided to help you build knowledge as to how your early emotional programming has contributed to your life journey as you know it today. You are encouraged to use the interactive exercises and journal activities to apply your learning to your own experiences and circumstances.

There are some stories in which the names and some situational details have been changed to protect the clients' privacy.

This book is not meant to take the place of sound professional psychological or medical advice, and is not intended in any way to diagnose, cure, or treat any type of medical illness or disease. For such diagnosis, please consult a qualified medical practitioner. Neither the author nor the publisher assumes any liability for possible adverse consequences as a result of the information contained herein.

TABLE OF CONTENTS

DEDICATION

This book is dedicated to the love of my life, Ted R. Battersby. You are my love, my lover, my protector, my champion, my cheerleader, and eternal soulmate…my T-Bear. You are the best husband, dad, and grandpa anyone could ask for.

Thank you for showing us the true meaning of unconditional love and unwavering commitment. You have always been the strong, yet gentle force behind all of us.

This work could not have happened without your encouragement and support. I only hope to bring as much love and magic into this world as you have brought into mine. I trust our next adventure together will be even more magical. Until we meet again, I will carry the love, courage, and strength of two hearts!

FOREWORD

Remember all the things you dreamed of having as a kid? What if you could really have it all?

From a very young age I, like most kids, had big dreams for what I wanted to become when I grew up—what my life would look like, what amazing things I would accomplish. I remember back to the early age of four, how fascinated I was by the circus—how exciting and magical it all was. My eyes were glued to the acrobats, knife-throwers, and tightrope walkers, but none more so than the magicians. I was completely mesmerized by their impossible-seeming tricks and illusions, and how they were able to convince the audience that making things magically appear and disappear was as simple as waving a wand and saying, "Abracadabra!" Then, POOF! It was so. How I wished to harness the powers of a real-life magician, sorcerer, or warlock... "Be careful what you wish for," they say.

Around the age of seven, I began watching the '60s TV show, *Bewitched* on syndication. It told the story of a mortal man who, unknowingly, married a witch. Though it was labeled a sitcom, for me, it felt more like an action drama; I was absolutely obsessed with it! With every episode I watched, I felt more and more sure that I could learn what it takes to acquire the magical powers I so desperately wanted. I modeled the witch character, Samantha, practicing relentlessly at twitching my nose, clicking my fingers, and repeating the words from her powerful spells. I thought that if I could just master this kind of magic, I could get people to do whatever I wanted and live the life of my dreams. Years passed, and the magic I'd dreamed of failed to materialize in my little world.

By the age of ten, my fixation transitioned from magic to heroic superpowers. Enter my obsession with the character Steve Austin from the TV show *The Six Million Dollar Man*. This sci-fi series was about a former astronaut whose body was "rebuilt" with bionic implants after a nearly fatal crash, giving him superhuman strength, speed, and vision. The opening theme of the show always got me so excited: "Steve Austin. Astronaut. A man barely alive. Gentlemen...we can rebuild him. We have the technology. We have the capability to build the world's first bionic man. Steve Austin will be that man—better than he was before. Better. Stronger. Faster." WOW! I envisioned that could be me, scaling tall buildings, squashing tennis balls with my bare hands, and running at 60 mph. If only I had his technology, life would be all I wanted it to be.

Throughout my teens, I manufactured many iterations of my desired "superhuman identity"—who I needed to become and what powers I needed to master to overcome life's difficulties and make a powerful impact on the world. I was relentless, daydreaming and strategizing about becoming a champion ice skater, world-class tennis player, creative artist, ingenious writer, savvy lawyer… Some of my identity visions lasted a few weeks, while others, several years.

What I realize now that I didn't know then is that there is a paradox that exists with being superhuman. Every superhero has an Achilles heel, often an unprocessed emotional trauma originating from their past, leaving them quite weak and vulnerable without their superpower. As a result, their life's purpose to serve humanity becomes a proverbial two-sided coin: the upside being known as the hero who saves the day, and the downside, spending a lifetime with unaddressed pain. A dual identity inevitably unfolds. Superman, the oldest, and arguably most iconic of the popular comic-book superheroes, was the "Man of Steel" in his superpower, but his alter ego, Clark Kent, was an adopted alien baby who was catapulted to Earth after his planet, Krypton exploded. His life was equally about "finding himself" as it was saving the Earth from violence and corruption.

Although my lofty superhuman visions kept my family amused, my commitment to see them through taught me to be quite decisive and determined. I graduated with a college degree majoring in law and built a successful $70 million company. On the flip side, I also developed a foreboding level of insecurity and fear of disappointment, sinking into some very dark periods of depression.

It's funny…as I look back now, I can't help but to be grateful. The experiences I deemed as struggles or failures helped me create massive results in many areas of my adult life. The active pursuit of learning and transforming I'd practiced as a child became a passion, internally driving me to apply my learnings immediately. This unconscious strategy was helping me generate a lot of success in my life, even though deep down, I spent most of my time feeling unconfident, self-conscious, and inadequate.

Over time, I ran into trouble when I began to compulsively "overuse" the strategies I had created, even if they weren't producing good results. This may sound harmless, but, my goodness, it sure led to a great deal of stress in my life—constantly pushing and forcing things to happen. When a strategy didn't work, I tended to simply apply more of the same thing, hoping for a different outcome. For most of my work life, I put in ridiculous hours, developing a very driven work ethic, and equally, various bouts of overwhelm and exhaustion. I became a "completion junkie," never stopping to smell the roses or just enjoy the journey. I had developed an all-or-nothing mentality, resulting in anything but the magical, superhuman life I had dreamt about. I knew something had to change but I didn't know where to begin. I had to find out what was wrong with me.

It was in my pursuit of finding answers when my path first crossed with Deb Battersby. She was speaking on stage at an event I was attending, and I remember being spellbound by the effortless way she presented her material. She moved across the stage delicately yet deliberately. Her gestures and body language were enigmatic and vivacious. Her humor, though sometimes self-deprecating, was quintessential and thoroughly entertaining. Her use of words and metaphors was absolutely masterful. Most importantly, her knowledge and expertise for her subject matter was nothing short of impressive. It was obvious she was following her vision and motivated by her mission and purpose. I became engrossed by her energy and enthusiasm to impact her audience in such a genuine, positive way. I also noticed she seemed to be equally intrigued with her audience, taking delight in eliciting an energetic response from us. Deb is acutely curious, highly intuitive, astute, flexible, creative, stoic, resilient, determined to make a difference, and masterful at utilizing and sharing her innate superpowers with the world. She is not a person to be trifled with. She takes a firm stance on most things, while remaining open, respectful, and fiercely nonjudgmental, making trust and rapport-building comfortable and easy.

Around 2008, I was introduced to Deb's proprietary and most distinguished FreedomPOINT method. I know of nothing else quite like it. P.O.I.N.T. is a five-step process that uncovers hidden subconscious emotional patterns which might prevent a person from living the fullest life they deserve, then transforms them through a gentle, non-intrusive method that's highly sensitive to one's personal emotional state. There is no judgement or assumption about "what comes up" in the conversation throughout the session because Deb's method is founded on a new paradigm: that every emotion exists to serve us in some way, no matter how harsh or painful it may seem.

When you consider emotions like hate, anger, overwhelm, or frustration, this paradigm may seem a bit illogical. You may naturally wonder how these emotions could be valuable or beneficial to you. That's where Deb comes in. As you will discover in this book, every emotion is like that two-sided coin with an upside and a downside. As children and throughout life, we are often taught to see the downside of certain emotions, yet we remain blind to how they are seeking to serve us in a very positive way. All emotions are intelligent, intentional, and valuable information to help us better navigate our journeys. As you will learn, P.O.I.N.T. takes you through a sequential process where the subconscious mind is unlocked and emotional patterns are communicated with, understood, then either released or upgraded to something that feels more supportive. Although I've seen astounding results come from just one session, sometimes it takes more than that to get to the center of the onion. That just means that, like the layers of an onion, emotions have a habit of layering upon themselves, oftentimes blocking or masking what's been sequestered at the subconscious core. Once an appreciation of an emotion's true intent is revealed, a domino effect can occur, collapsing all the other patterns which have been piled on top of or around it.

There is no judgment or discrimination in the P.O.I.N.T. method. It's a safe, highly confidential, comforting process where time just kind of "stands still." Emotions are communicated and conversed with in the first person to obtain the information needed to "solve the emotion pattern puzzle." Furthermore, the client's past deeds, behaviors, history, or beliefs are albeit irrelevant to the process. Identifying, understanding, and confronting how the pattern makes you feel is the beginning to experiencing your own emotional freedom.

I have been fortunate to have experienced many of my own FreedomPOINT sessions. I often contact Deb to let her know "It's time for a tune up!" because there is always another level of patterns to explore and work through. You never know what's going to "show up," and sometimes the results are revealed over time versus experienced immediately, but there's always a shift that happens on a cellular level. Once this happens, the way you typically behaved in a past situation can be radically transformed forever. Old, unconscious reactions to distressing circumstances can be neutralized, and new meanings come to the fore. FreedomPOINT is literally a life-changing experience. As you will read in this book, there are clear, simple steps which empower you to sharpen your own awareness and resourcefulness around your emotional patterns.

There's a saying that people come into your life for a reason, a season, or a lifetime. How true. Since our first encounter and over the years that have followed, my path has continued to cross with Deb's at seminars and events across the globe. There's no doubt we were destined to strike up and develop a magical and enduring friendship. "Debz," as she became fondly known by her ever-growing fan and client base, is a remarkable woman. Even after 15 years, I count her my dearest friend in the world. She is also my personal coach, consultant to my expanding business, and general all-purpose resource for just about anything.

Deb has a show reel of accomplishments including Master Trainer, Personal Coach, Real Estate Sales Guru, NLP Master Practitioner, and of course, loving wife and mother. She has spent decades investing in her own personal development to be of service to humankind, which is a testament to her commitment of holding herself to the highest possible standard in any endeavor she pursues. I've heard it takes 10,000 hours of practical application to reach the status of "expert" in anything; I am sure Deb has racked up at least ten times that number as it relates to her diverse education and personal development.

I thoroughly recommend FreedomPOINT to any therapist or coach who's keen to utilize Deb's proven, cutting-edge technology. I also recommend it to entrepreneurs and business leaders as a tool to lead, communicate, and influence more effectively. Indeed, every family can benefit from her method as well!

One of my most memorable P.O.I.N.T. sessions with "Debz" occurred on a warm, sunny afternoon during the fall of 2017. I remember the sky was incredibly clear that day, and the ocean near my house was the deepest shade of jade green I had ever seen. The scene was set for something incredible, it seemed. I had recently emerged from a particularly dark emotional period in my life, and we had worked on (and resolved) several underlying patterns prior to this particular session. Little did I know at the time that my "alter ego" would come forth at the very end of that session with the creation and installation of a brand-new identity. Neither of us were expecting this to happen; it just showed up—I guess it was time. My new superhero identity, which I named "MX" was born and unleashed on the world at that very moment while I was lying on my lounge! "MX" serves me to this day and is an intrinsic part of practically everything I do. At the time, it only felt like a millimeter shift in my psyche, like the incision of a tiny scalpel, but the magic that has shown up in my life since then is nothing short of spectacular. My personal life has never been better or more fulfilling, my business is thriving and more profitable than ever. I still experience challenges and pain, of course—I'm human—but my ability to respond in times of trial is massively improved. I enjoy life like never before, genuinely thriving in the gratitude for all the blessings I have. I guess you could say I'm leading a pretty magical life after all.

I know you will enjoy this book, as it represents the pinnacle of Deb's life's work and expertise. Like *The Six Million Dollar Man*, Deb has developed the technology through FreedomPOINT to rebuild your emotional patterns and reconnect you with your innate superpowers, which is indeed raising the consciousness of our planet in a tremendous, impactful way.

Thank you for being my secret weapon, Debz!

Mark Hunter

CEO, Hunter Express

ACKNOWLEDGMENTS

I would like to acknowledge the work of the following individuals for their contributions to the field of personal development, human potential, and life transformation. I'm extremely grateful to have studied and worked personally with several of them.

Dr. Richard Bandler, Brandon Bays, Jack Canfield, Deepak Chopra, M.D., Sonia Choquette, PhD, Master Stephen Co, Robert Dilts, Dr. Joe Dispenza, Dr. Wayne W. Dyer, Werner Erhard, Dr. John Grinder, Dr. David Hawkins, Louise Hay, Gay Hendricks, PhD, Katie Hendricks, PhD, BC-DMT, Napoleon Hill, Byron Katie, Bruce Lipton, PhD, Maxwell Maltz, M.D., F.I.C.S., Bob Proctor, Tony Robbins, Jim Rohn, Michael Singer, Brian Tracy, Marianne Williamson

A special thanks goes to Tony Robbins for 30 years of unique opportunities, formidable challenges, and expansive growth! It has been a privilege to be immersed in this leadership program, sharing a path of self-discovery and service with amazing souls from around the world.

I'd also like to thank my angels: the many family members, friends, and colleagues who have been avid supporters in helping me explore and evolve this work. Much gratitude goes to Deb Collins for making our online courses a reality. Most importantly, my deepest thanks go to the hundreds of clients and students who have been essential to the inspiration and intrigue that kept me curious and hungry to learn more about what was possible when engaging the wisdom beyond the conscious mind.

I'm especially grateful to my husband Ted, my son Stephen, and my daughter Erin for being a constant source of love, acceptance, support, encouragement, and inspiration.

What To Expect

"Nature's message was always there and for us to see. It was written on the wings of butterflies."

—*Kjell B. Sandved*

THE FACT THAT you chose this book (or, as I like to believe, the book chose you) means there's a good chance that directly or indirectly, you're either experiencing some difficulty moving through life in an easy way, it's time to pivot and go in a new direction, or something needs to change, even if you don't know what it is. Regardless of your reason, you know it's time to uplevel your life. (Sound familiar?) It's no secret we're living in a time of mass awakening—awakening to who we truly are at our core and to the purpose we're here to serve on this planet. Although I have mentored and coached thousands of people in their quest for next-level achievement and relief from emotional and physical pain, I am, perhaps like you, a perpetual student of human behavior and transformation. I want to know the depths of human potential and how to unlock the greater capacity we somehow know is there, lying quietly within us, waiting to be liberated. That's why we can get so frustrated with the emotion patterns that limit us; we know we are capable of so much more.

We are all growing and evolving every day, yet we often lose sight of who we truly are because of who we've unconsciously become. We have been taught to distrust our emotional communication system, blocking the intelligent, intentional messages being delivered from the subconscious mind. In this book, you are about to embark on a journey home—home to the truth of your pure essence.

Who would you be if you could release your blocks and limiting beliefs?

Who would you be without associating yourself with the false labels you've been assigned through the opinions and influences of others?

Who would you be without the restrictive emotion patterns that seem to keep you stuck, repeating the same old programs over and over again?

Perhaps the better question is, "Who *could* you be?"

The discovery I want to share with you in this book is the brilliance of the emotional communication system of the subconscious mind to release or transform any behavioral pattern. The genius of this resource that each of us has access to never ceases to amaze me. It continually delivers new insights and understandings with every client session.

In the following pages, you will notice these words used interchangeably: thoughts, feelings, emotions, beliefs, behaviors, habits, patterns, as they each represent the energy and information we're looking to transform. They all play an intricate part of your inner communication system.

FreedomPOINT emerged from my own desire to understand, heal, and transform the emotions that hold us back from living life to its fullest, most beautiful, and most authentic potential. Fear, worry, confusion, depression, anxiety, low self-esteem, unworthiness…these are emotions that can cause doubt in our inner ability to thrive in the world. These emotional responses can become habits and patterns that are difficult to shake no matter how hard we try. Over time, they simmer under the surface of our psyche keeping us trapped in identities that are anything but who we were meant to be. It's easy to believe our emotion patterns are "who we are," yet nothing could be further from the truth. Our beliefs, feelings, and behaviors are not who we are; they are merely a product of unconscious modeling and conditioning. And this, we can transform!

I developed the FreedomPOINT method to provide you with the tools that will enable you to tap into your true potential and achieve the emotional liberation you've been searching for. This book will help you:

~ appreciate the emotions you think are "negative" or "bad"
~ understand that every emotion pattern you have is serving you in an intentional way
~ identify the upside and downside to your emotion patterns
~ learn the fundamentals of your inner communication system
~ discover the limitless power and genius of your subconscious mind
~ shift unwanted patterns to ones that better serve and support you
~ recognize the brilliance of your protective emotion patterns
~ negotiate with your subconscious mind to upgrade your vast matrix of emotion patterns

Beyond the Introduction, this book is presented in four parts:

PART I: The Starting POINT

In Part I, you will be taken on an introspective journey of self-discovery, building an understanding of how your beliefs and patterns were formed and how you can unlock the door to living the life you really want.

PART II: P.O.I.N.T.ing the Way to Emotional Transformation

Part II will guide you through my five-step P.O.I.N.T. method designed to release the emotion patterns that are holding you back from transforming your life into the one you most want to live.

* *Although Part II is written toward the practitioner-client perspective, you will have the opportunity to implement each step for your own personal FreedomPOINT journey in Part IV.*

PART III: Client Transformation Stories

In Part III, you will be introduced to the transformational stories of some of my clients who have overcome emotion patterns such as anxiety, perfectionism, fear of not being enough, paranoia, depression, and many others. Through these powerful stories, you may identify with some of the patterns in your own life, and you will have the opportunity to journal in personal self-reflection after each one.

PART IV: Your P.O.I.N.T. Journey

In Part IV, you will be guided to explore your own personal transformation journey using the FreedomPOINT five-step method. You will learn to use automatic writing and journaling to take yourself through a personal FreedomPOINT session.

Helpful Resources

Following Part IV, I have provided some helpful tools and resources to assist you with your transformational journey.

POINTers

Periodically throughout the book, you will be invited to take a pause for personal reflection through POINTers. These are quotes, stand-out statements, or key takeaways designed to help you generate a deeper understanding about the P.O.I.N.T. method and how it can contribute to living the life you really want. You will also have the opportunity to build a deeper awareness of your own emotion patterns through journaling exercises.

A Little Bit About "ME"

Okay…you're about to dig in, and I realize you may be wondering, is this book really for me? Well, that's a perfectly good question, so let's talk about YOU as a "ME" for a moment. As you approach the information, concepts, and principles throughout the following pages, it's important to recognize that to achieve transformation, you can only start from where you are. Your identity, or your ME, is a direct result of your unique, personal life experiences. The perspective of your ME is packed with the people, places, memories, stories, and emotional events which have literally shaped the person who's reading this book right now! Your ME consists of countless factors ranging from the DNA that is your genetic makeup to the reason you'll choose chocolate cake over apple pie for dessert. (I'll explain that later.)

Simply put, your ME is your identity; it's what you believe about who you are and what you're capable of, and it's 100% transformable.

ME Times 3

There are three MEs (or identities) that everyone has: a Past ME, Current ME, and Ideal ME. As you will learn, there is an intricate web of scientific, energetic, and behavioral factors which have been expertly spun and woven together by your Past ME to create your Current ME—the ME who is reading this book. FreedomPOINT will help you better understand how you developed into your Current ME over time, and most importantly, how you can transform the emotion patterns that are holding you back and amplify the ones that will propel you toward becoming your Ideal ME.

Choosing a Lens

The ME Lens

If you've chosen to read this book through the lens of your "self," I can safely assume you have some level of interest in achieving emotional freedom in your own life or in the life of a loved one. The stories and situational examples used in this book will likely create some beautiful "ME too!" moments for you, as you reflect on your own personal journey. They may also stir up some discomfort; after all, life doesn't just serve up roses and rainbows, right? Although you may stumble through some of the weeds of your Past ME, I promise you there's a bountifully blooming garden that awaits you at the end of this book—just stick with me!

One of my favorite Bible passages in 1 Corinthians tells us that God does not call the qualified; He qualifies the called. Many of my clients and colleagues who have learned about FreedomPOINT have gone on to become certified FreedomPOINT practitioners, and there will be more information in the Helpful Resources section if you also feel called to join me in facilitating this work.

The Coach Lens

If you've chosen to read this book through the lens of a coach, therapist, or healing practitioner and have been playing on the personal development playground for a while, you may find some of the scientific, energetic, and behavioral principles familiar. However, unweaving the web of emotions, thoughts, beliefs, and patterns in a way that contributes to understanding and applying the FreedomPOINT method in Part II will undoubtedly be a new experience for you. It will also enable you to explore new avenues to guide your clients, as I will be guiding you.

You can use the Coach lens and the ME lens simultaneously or read the book again from a fresh perspective.

Open Your Mind

"Minds are like parachutes; they only function when open."
—*Thomas Dewar*

As a success coach, Master Practitioner in neurolinguistics and neuro-associative conditioning, and a certified hypnotherapist, I've studied and mentored with some of the world's most renowned life coaches, wellness practitioners, and business strategists, using many proven mindset methodologies in my FreedomPOINT method to help others create lasting life transformation. This work is my passion, my joy, my gift, and my service to my fellow freedom seekers. My passion and my commitment are to help you achieve the emotional transformation you've been searching for. True freedom is about living the authentic truth of your ME. The guide to inner freedom you're about to embark on is based on many years of my direct experience in designing, developing, and facilitating the FreedomPOINT method through thousands of client sessions.

This book contains many scientific, energetic, behavioral, and even spiritual truths, some of which you may not personally align with, and that's okay. My challenge to you is a simple one: let go of the "I know" mindset before you turn the page.

Make the decision to pull the ripcord, open your mind, and get ready to discover *your* truth.

INTRODUCTION

"I must be ready now..."

INTRODUCTION

"I must be ready now..."

"Adding wings to caterpillars does not create butterflies, it creates awkward and dysfunctional caterpillars. Butterflies are created through transformation."

—*Stephanie Marshall*

M Y PERSONAL DEVELOPMENT journey began back in the early 1980s, but my FreedomPOINT adventure began with a fortuitous car accident on June 1, 2000. I was driving down Golf Road in Schaumburg, IL when I received a phone call from a spiritual teacher who had been referred to me by a mutual friend. I answered, "Oh my gosh, we've been playing phone tag for weeks...*I must be ready now!*" In that split second, I was blindsided by a car that crashed into the passenger side of my sedan. Rather than rushing straight to the hospital or to a chiropractor, I went home to lie down. A few hours later, the entire right side of my body, including my brain, began to spasm. I can't recall how long it lasted, but I remember lying still in bed, just observing all that was happening to me. When I woke up the next day, everything seemed strangely and drastically different.

I hopped into my husband's SUV and had been driving for about 15 minutes when suddenly, I realized my awareness of everything happening around me had become extremely heightened. I initially rationalized my experience, expecting my nervous system would be on hyper-alert having just been plowed into the day before. As I continued driving, however, I was noticing things that could potentially impact or interact with me, yet there was no "space" between the *seeing* and the *knowing*. As someone who consistently uses deductive reasoning (if "this" happens, then "this" is likely to happen), I'm always looking for the cause and effect of a situation. Yet, on that particular day, I was able to "see" things and have an instant "knowing" of their potential, with no thought in between. Never before had I had that kind of experience: *seeing and knowing with no thinking in between.* Over the following days, weeks, and months, I began to "see" emotional patterns in the same way—observing emotion triggers and almost immediately "knowing" the trajectory they would take. For example, within a couple of seconds, I could observe the emotion of "unmet expectations," then literally watch that emotion begin to domino, falling into disappointment, then sadness, then hurt, then anger, then resentment... That was the beginning of my FreedomPOINT mission.

The Road to Transformation

For at least ten years prior to my "accident," I had already been quite fascinated with transformative emotional experiences, becoming heavily involved in the Tony Robbins organization, as well as studying neurolinguistics and neuro-associative conditioning. With each event I attended and through my own personal study, I began to wonder why some people could effectively transform their patterns, while others, although they worked hard at creating change, never experienced lasting results. It was like they were trying to pin on their butterfly wings but were still caterpillars. I became more and more curious about discovering the factors that led to creating lasting transformation consistently. Back then, it seemed like it was somewhat random; a group of people could go through the same experience, some achieving transformation, some not. One person may have received intense intellectual insights, and they were indeed motivated to make a change, but *they weren't transformed.*

There's a subtle yet outcome-altering distinction between "making a change" and "achieving transformation." Let me explain. The word "change" means to make something different. Interestingly, many of the synonyms for change are words that begin with the prefix "re": redo, refashion, remake, revamp, revise, rework, reform. The prefix "re" is attached to roots or words to form verbs or nouns referring to "action in a backward direction, intended to undo or reverse a situation, to do over again, or bring back."

Now, let's look at the word "transform." Transform means "to go beyond form without altering the value"—*going beyond your form.* Synonyms include words like alchemize, make over, convert, transmute, transpose. The prefix "trans" is attached to root words making verbs which refer to "movement or carrying from one place to another," as well as making adjectives referring to "crossing, going beyond or on the other side of (something)."

So, what the heck does all this heady vocabulary have to do with emotional healing? The truth is, I've seen countless therapeutic and coaching methods, as I'm sure you have too, which promise to *help you make positive changes* to live a happier, more fulfilling life. I've even participated in my fair share of self-help seminars, workshops, and online programs which taught me some great tips on how to go about *changing* my thought processes and behavior patterns, but after a while, I noticed that many of my deeply rooted emotional wounds would eventually resurface, and the personal development tips I'd learned were like a small band-aid placed over a much bigger wound. I realized that in order to experience results that make a *lasting difference* in your emotional well-being, achieving transformation from the inside out is necessary.

What We Want to Transform

Some time ago, I attended a lecture where a neuroscientist professed approximately 95% of what we do every day is directed by subconscious and unconscious programs. In the beginning phase of my work, I thought what I was doing was "unraveling" emotion patterns, but over time, FreedomPOINT became more about transforming the underlying patterns etched into the subconscious—the ones running on autopilot. If 95% of what we do is driven by subconscious programming, then to create real transformation, I would have to learn how to affect this system—to transform the patterns that hold us back into ones that amplify our strengths and unleash our authentic selves. I needed to figure out how to "clear the cache" of subconscious programs, and like the character Neo in my favorite movie *The Matrix*, disrupt the illusion of limitation we have come to believe and accept. My work would have to change the matrix.

It's important to mention that when working with the subconscious, we are working with established neurological patterns and strategies that are, in essence, simply energy and information. Basic quantum theory… everything is energy and information. The energy and information presents in myriad ways—thoughts, feelings, emotions, beliefs, behaviors, habits, language pattens, metaphors…all of which can be happening separately, simultaneously, or as part of a chain reaction.

In this book, you will learn that certain information can make us "feel" good, bad, or neutral, yet the information itself ALWAYS has a positive intent. No matter how they make you "feel," your feelings, emotions, and beliefs are not the enemy—ever. They are here to serve you and always have your back. Over the course of your life, you have developed and stored specific ways to navigate, cope with, and respond to what's happening in your world. With FreedomPOINT, the ultimate goal is to identify and transform the energy and information strategies that are no longer working for you, without judgment.

Trust Your Ability to Transform

> *"When a tongue speaks the truth, every cell in creation testifies."*
> —*Vujika Andrich*

We are born with an emotional communication system miraculously and flawlessly designed. It filters our external and internal environments so we can respond efficiently, effectively, and appropriately to any given situation. Thank goodness for us, no one else needs to affirm or deny our truth. However, learning to trust the truth that lives inside takes practice. Trusting our internal communication system is a process designed to guide us through thoughts, choices, beliefs, and behaviors. So, what is this emotional guidance system, exactly? Our emotional guidance system is an *inner intelligence* that lets us know when we're on track and when we're off. Oftentimes, we override the subtle pings coming from our own guidance system to stick to the beliefs stemming from our past experiences. And once we decide that something is true, it becomes quite difficult to convince ourselves otherwise.

Once while attending a seminar, I had a chance encounter with a beautiful soul who shared some of her poetry with me. There was one line, a single sentence, I will never forget because it became an integral part of my ability and strategy to discern truth: "When a tongue speaks the truth, every cell in creation testifies."

That one little sentence hit me like a bolt of lightning; I knew exactly what she meant. The body responds to truth in very specific ways. Goosebumps, chills, hair standing up on the arms or neck are confirmations of truth. We can also do muscle testing to validate truth, where the muscles go weak in the introduction of falsehood and go strong with the introduction of truth.

We are so conditioned to look externally for validation and justification of who we are, what we believe, and what we're capable of, when all we really need can be found right inside of us—inside of our very bodies. The testimony of truth is right there in our cells! When I see goosebumps pop up on my arms or feel shivers running down my spine, these are my cells testifying that they have heard and felt the truth. Since then, I've always looked for truth that resonates on that level—from the inside out. As you learn the FreedomPOINT method, I expect you will experience many of your own "confirmations of truth."

> *"There is nothing in a caterpillar that tells you it's going to be a butterfly."*   —*R. Buckminster Fuller*

As children, we learn about the miraculous process by which a caterpillar transforms into a butterfly. A hungry caterpillar hatches from an egg and stuffs itself with leaves, getting fatter and fatter as it munches its way through life. Eventually, the caterpillar stops eating, sheds its skin, hangs upside down from a twig or leaf, and spins itself into a safe, silky cocoon. Within its protective casing, the caterpillar radically transforms its body and emerges as a beautiful butterfly. One stage at a time, the caterpillar is compelled to transform toward its highest evolution. This creature already has the inner intelligence of its natural, divine creation to ensure it becomes the butterfly it was always born to be.

You, too, have this same inner intelligence—an embedded blueprint to become your most wonderful, evolved self. At the same time, you also have the option to stay small, distrusting the intelligence of your emotional guidance system. When you take on the biases and judgments of others, you steer away from the divine essence of your true Ideal ME, remaining as the fat, hungry caterpillar your whole life. Your past is not indicative of your future.

This book isn't about "changing" behaviors. This book is about revealing the inner genius of your own communication system via the subconscious and learning how to work with it to achieve powerful growth and personal transformation. The FreedomPOINT method is unique in that it takes you *beyond behavioral change* and straight to "transformation," enabling you to literally replace stuck patterns of emotion-thought bonds and programs with new ones that support you in discovering the truth of who you were always meant to be. And yes...IT IS POSSIBLE!

Trust and believe in your ability to transform.

I believe that by consistently pondering the question, "What's the difference between conditioned change and true transformation?" I actually *invited* that car accident into my life. I also believe it was one of the greatest gifts I've ever been given. It is that question that ushered in the event which allowed my brain to see things differently, through an altered state of consciousness and perspective. "Seeing" emotion patterns, uncovering their intention, and negotiating with them to guide others through conversation with their subconscious mind became my life's work and passion. I didn't know it then, but that car accident was perhaps the most profound butterfly moment of my life; it gave me my wings.

PART I

The Starting POINT

PART I

The Starting POINT

"How does one become a butterfly? You have to want to learn to fly so much that you are willing to give up being a caterpillar."

—*Trina Paulus*

Pain Points

Whenever I begin working with a client to uncover which emotional patterns are causing difficulty in their life, oftentimes they rattle off a laundry list of events that happened to them attempting to explain why they are where they are.

"My divorce was finalized last month..."

"I'm taking care of an elderly, sick parent…"

"My daughter moved back in with her two kids…"

"My new boss is unreasonable and the stress at work is too much to handle…"

Does this sound familiar? Haven't we all unknowingly prefaced our emotion patterns with a story? Of course, we have. Yet, despite all the explaining and justifying of our current conditions, we still want to better understand ourselves—the ME behind it all. We ask ourselves, "Who am I? Why am I like this? How did I get here? Where do I go from here?" If we could only figure these things out, we could change a few things and live more comfortably inside ourselves and show up more confidently in the world.

Your ME is packed with people, places, memories, stories, desires, and events that are *unique to your life journey*. We spend countless hours reliving the past—the memories and experiences of disappointment, upset, and failure—attempting to understand *what's* holding us back, *why* it's holding us back, and *how* it's screwing up our lives—all so we can somehow find a way to "get over it and get on with it."

In my many years of guiding people through FreedomPOINT, the emotional patterns people describe most often result from an interpretation of the past or projection of the future, neither of which can be totally accurate. These interpretations and projections become the basis of their reality and influence how they filter all the information from their environment. So, for them, it has become a fixed reality—the life of their Current ME—forever. Of course, whatever circumstances people experience are true for them, but it is the *meaning they give* to these situations that shapes their current reality.

Your Life as a Movie

Our emotional responses are controlled as much by the conditioning of our Past ME as they are by the circumstances of our Current ME. The emotional triggers imprinted from childhood largely determined our choices, decisions, and direction in life. Writing one scene at a time, we've scripted a movie about ourselves. We've watched it over and over, thousands of times, reinforcing the story we've told about ourselves. The unfortunate reality is the scenes in our movie include countless experiences that were misunderstood and misinterpreted, resulting in distortions and misconceptions; thus, we accepted them as "truth" without conscious understanding, consent, or permission. These patterns are the operating system we've created to run our lives. They contain our beliefs about the world and our definition of "ME." From there, we wrote, directed, and produced our movie. It's how we managed to make sense of our lives and find a way of fitting into the world we live in.

In the same way a child has a bad dream and believes it to be real, adults live (and relive) their past hurts and fears as if these "bad dreams" are happening now. By replaying bad dreams and old movies, we get trapped (unknowingly) in a painful script—a movie whose plot is not the love story we want for our lives. The propensity to focus on the past ties us to an old version of ourselves, often keeping us from moving forward in the ways we want to. And when we do move forward, we're usually slugging along some heavy emotional baggage along with us.

It is wise to remember, two people who experience the same set of circumstances can put radically different spins on what happened, and consequently, how the experience impacted them. Imagine two brothers who spent their early years with an abusive, alcoholic father who ended up in jail. One of the sons became a drug addict and spent some time in jail; the other son became a very successful business owner who did a lot of volunteer work to help the less fortunate of his community. When asked why each of them took the path they did, they both answered, "With a father like mine, what choice did I have?"

What's holding us back from experiencing our most joyful and fulfilled lives has little or nothing to do with our actual life events. What holds us back are the feelings and emotions *attached* to those events. They dwell inside us, holding on for dear life, unwilling to let go, and every time we dredge up those unpleasant memories—the scenes from our life move—we reinforce the feelings telling us something is wrong, and we better do something to fix it.

POINTer

The thoughts and beliefs you hold about who you are and how you got that way are relevant, indeed. But how you feel about what you think is either your jailer or your liberator.

How Did We Get Here?

> *"Cut a chrysalis open, and you will find a rotting caterpillar. What you will never find is that mythical creature, half caterpillar, half butterfly, a fit emblem for the human soul, for those whose cast of mind leads them to seek such emblems. No, the process of transformation consists almost entirely of decay."*
> —Pat Barker

I was working with a client (I'll call her Judy) who was stressed out of her gourd. Her need for everything to be perfect, including herself, was creating enormous stress, anxiety, and worry. All of this was adding fuel to the underlying fear of not being enough. It was late fall, and the holidays were fast approaching. In our first session, Judy shared how much she dreaded the Thanksgiving holidays but didn't really understand why. The closer November came, the more stress and anxiety she felt. She became unusually impatient and intolerant and found herself snapping at family and friends without much provocation. As we explored this pattern a little deeper, she told me a story about baking apple pies with her mother when she was a child. From the time Judy was a little girl, her mother would get up early on Thanksgiving morning to make breakfast and bake a fresh apple pie from scratch. And every year, without fail, Judy was summoned to the kitchen to help, having to listen to her mother repeat the same instructions about how to make her great-grandmother's "perfect apple pie."

Judy and her mother cut up the apples and mixed the cinnamon and sugar—that was the easy part. The grand finale of it all was recreating great-grandma's famous crust. Great skill and care went into achieving the right amount of wetness of the dough, how much flour to use in dusting the countertop and coating the rolling pin, how many times to roll the dough in multiple directions to get it just thin enough to nestle gently into the pie pan without tearing, yet still thick enough to make those little thumbprint divots around the top edge.

As Judy recounted this story, she commented on the level of meticulousness that her mother required of her in baking that perfect apple pie. Should any part of the process go wrong, the pie would be considered an epic failure. If the crust was too soggy on the bottom or too dark around the edges...if the apples were too firm or if there was too much cinnamon added...it wouldn't have lived up to the standard that had been followed for decades. When I asked Judy, *"How does that story make you feel?"* she expressed how pressured she felt having to do everything perfectly to avoid her mother's disappointment.

One Thanksgiving, Judy had over-rolled the crust with the rolling pin, and as she began to lay it into the pie pan, the crust began to tear. She remembered her mother looking over her shoulder, shaking her head in disappointment, pushing her out of the way and saying, "You're hopeless. This pie isn't going to turn out right." Just as her mother predicted, the pie turned out far from perfect. When it was time for dessert, the pie was presented to the family with an embarrassment-filled apology from her mother, leaving Judy feeling like a complete failure. Even as she retold the story to me many years later, her feelings of anxiety, shame, disappointment, and rejection were as alive for her as they had been on that fateful Thanksgiving Day.

Judy discovered that the event of screwing up the apple pie left a deep emotional wound of being a screw-up. Reliving the pie experience every Thanksgiving rolled into a lifetime of anxiety and perfectionism that became downright debilitating at times, particularly around the holidays. Through our session, Judy pinpointed the event at the core of her unmanageable anxiety, and now she could finally let it go.

Is it possible that this one little event could have set Judy on a path of struggling to be perfect in every area of her life—perfect for her boss, perfect for her co-workers, even perfect for her friends and in her romantic relationships? The imperfect apple pie generated such emotional distress, it caused Judy to develop the belief that nothing she did would ever be seen as good enough. Deep down inside, her belief that "if the pie's not perfect, it's not good enough" became "if *I'm* not perfect, *I'm* not good enough." Hence, a lifelong pattern of trying to be perfect was set in motion.

The most dramatic downside of this pattern is, if anything can be made even a little smidge better, it isn't perfect, and it never will be. So, in essence, perfection is not achievable; it's a moving target. Anxiety and stress were inevitable because Judy was pursuing an impossible goal: always striving for perfection in every area of her life.

Judy is not alone. We all have behavior patterns that originated from highly emotional experiences from our childhood years. Memories and the corresponding emotions from those events can be as real and vivid today as they were at the time they originally happened. The pattern is therefore well established in the nervous system and becomes an automatic go-to when any situation even remotely resembling the old experience shows up. Emotion, reaction, and behavior are programmed; autopilot is set.

Installing Your Programs

You are humanly designed to observe and model the world around you—the people, events, and experiences in your environment—and you automatically absorb that information like a sponge as a young child. It's how you learn to "fit in." Day in and day out, the people, events, and experiences you encounter cause situational, emotional reactions that are stamped, or imprinted into your subconscious mind.

Most of our programming happens before the age of seven. Scientists propose the subconscious mind has no filters before the ages of seven or eight; it's wide open to be trained. This means it accepts everything it's given without question or analysis. A young child is unable to make logical sense of situations and emotions because the brain hasn't developed or matured enough to consciously consider how to deal with stressful emotions. That's why we see toddlers throwing tantrums without really knowing why they're so distraught. During this period, we are at the emotional mercy of others' opinions, judgments, labels, assumptions, and accusations. "You're stupid; you're smart; you're beautiful; you're ugly; you're lovable; you're unlovable; you're a troublemaker"—all are accepted as truth. Generally, the things we see and hear the most, or which come from the people we most expect to be looking out for us, have the greatest impact. It is only after the age of eight when the subconscious mind begins to develop the ability to evaluate information that comes at us or to us. This is when we can begin to reject some of the things presented to us. We can say, "That doesn't make sense" or "I don't agree." Prior to that, everything lands in the subconscious as absolute truth.

Living the Labels

"Everybody knows what a caterpillar is, and it doesn't look anything like a butterfly." —*Lynn Margulis*

Your outer reality is influenced by the internal beliefs you hold as "true" about your Current ME. Most people don't even realize the barrage of labels that have been stuck to them by parents, friends, teachers, schoolmates, spouses, bosses… The ability to experience the world directly and objectively has been all but stripped away. We are taught to compare, classify, and categorize people rather than look intentionally for their true nature and believe the best about them and ourselves. People's opinions and judgments about us are simply that; they are not who we are. Stripping away the layers of labels is like peeling back an onion, one layer at a time.

In a recent client session, "Rita" was struggling to break through a new income level in her network marketing business. What showed up for her was the feeling of "undeserving," more specifically, "you don't deserve it." This feeling was triggered by a voice in her head that kept saying, "You don't deserve it." Upon further exploration, we discovered it wasn't her voice at all; it was the voice of a second-grade classmate who was taunting her on the playground over 30 years ago. To loosen the grip of this decades-old program, we first examined what the possible upside/benefit was that had come from it. You may scoff and think, what the heck could be good about thinking "you don't deserve it?" Here's the part that's counterintuitive: in Rita's case, the upside was "determination" and "drive." She had to prove (to herself and everyone else) she was worthy of every success she achieved. Rita recreated the scene by visualizing herself on that playground and receiving those words from her classmate, responding with "No, thank you," and giving them back to her. Her sense of freedom went through the roof as she let go of this old language pattern and the feelings that were associated with it. She had no trouble reaching even higher income targets in the months that followed.

Remember the nursery rhyme, "Sticks and stones may break my bones, but words will never hurt me." The truth is, broken bones heal but the wounds from words can fester for a lifetime.

The formulation of who we are—our ME—is heavily impacted by the words spoken to us or about us during those impressionable years. It is the beginning of shaping our beliefs about what we deserve or don't deserve, what we can have or not have, and who we can be or not be.

Ropes of Belief

The story of the Baby Elephant Syndrome is a beautiful way to think about mindset and the power of your beliefs. A baby elephant is tied to a tree with a rope that's strong enough to keep it from breaking free. As the elephant grows bigger and stronger, it is conditioned to believe it can never escape, so while the elephant is now physically strong enough to uproot the entire tree, because of its beliefs through repetitive conditioning, it allows the same rope to keep it captive. The previously failed attempts to break free causes the elephant to believe the bonds are simply unbreakable. Because of habitual conditioning, the grown elephant won't make the slightest effort to escape. It has the power to break free at any time, but because it was conditioned to *believe* the rope is stronger, the rope will forever keep the elephant stuck right where it is.

The complexity of the human psyche is quite astounding. As human beings, we are no different than the elephant except for one thing: we can *choose* to reject self-imposed boundaries and limitations, as well as the labels previously accepted by our Past ME.

"Everything we hear is an opinion, not a fact. Everything we see is a perspective, not the truth." —Marcus Aurelius

I had my own experience with labels, assumptions, and accusations back in elementary school. It started when I was in sixth grade. My new Math teacher, "Mr. T." had my brother Rob in his class the previous year. It would be an understatement to say they didn't get along. Mr. T. didn't like my brother and had made up his mind he wasn't going to like me either. In his mind, I was already a troublemaker even though he'd never met me.

In the first week of the new semester, I was in Mr. T's class when a patrol boy came to report a student for misbehavior on the school grounds. (Patrol boys and girls were upperclassmen who served as crossing guards and playground supervisors. They had the authority to report students to their teachers if the student was deemed to be out of line.) The patrol boy came into the classroom and said to Mr. T., "Barbara picked a fight with another girl on the playground this morning." Mr. T. looked at me and said, "Petway (my maiden name), I knew you were going to be trouble. Go to the principal's office right now." Through my tears and humiliation, all I could muster was, "My name isn't Barbara." His response was, "I know you're trouble and can't be trusted." I felt confused, embarrassed, falsely accused, hurt, and angry. I hadn't started a fight with anyone. I wasn't a troublemaker; in fact, I was a quiet, shy, nerdy, straight-A student who loved school and loved to achieve, but he couldn't see that because he had already labeled me as something else.

That day, I accepted the emotion pattern of "I have to prove myself." This pattern is much like Judy's perfectionism pattern in that there is no way to win because there is never enough "proof." Two years later, I was in my last year of elementary school (eighth grade) and Mr. T. was my homeroom teacher. A few of my classmates nominated me to run for president of our graduating class. To be an eligible candidate, you were required to have at least a B average and couldn't have any disciplinary checks on your report card. During that particular marking period, Mr. T. gave me a check for being disruptive in class which disqualified me as a candidate to run for class president. I was devastated! I'd never had a negative check mark before, and now I was ineligible to run for office. He later accused me, in front of the whole class, of cheating on the high school advanced placement exams when I scored the highest marks in our class. Needless to say, Mr. T. never changed his assumptions about me. Everything I had done to prove I was a good kid and conscientious student wasn't enough proof. Over the coming years, my "need to prove" pattern became even more intense.

> *"The problem with making assumptions is that we believe they are the truth."* —*Don Miguel Ruiz*

The assumptions people make, and the things people say about us and to us can be demoralizing and even devastating in their impact. My experience with Mr. T. undermined my self-belief and eroded my confidence for a time; however, there was a definite upside to this whole scenario. I learned to question things. No one is infallible; people in positions of authority are not always right and sometimes misuse their power. I became someone who could and would challenge authority when it was being abused or was abusive to me or others. I also learned that I am the one who gets to decide what's true about ME. Over time, I began to recognize all the *benefits* that came from my "need to prove" pattern.

Later in the book, you're going to see how these seemingly limiting patterns of language, belief, emotion, and behavior all have an upside: a positive intent and desirable benefits. You'll also learn how to identify the downside and work with the subconscious mind to create better strategies that enhance the intended upside and eliminate the downside. For now, let's dive a little deeper into understanding the mind.

It's All in Your Mind

"We are infected by our own misunderstanding of how our own minds work." —Kevin Kelly

I would add to Kevin Kelly's quote that "we are also infected by our own misunderstanding of how our emotions work."

The quest for understanding and treating emotions reaches back many hundreds of years. With all the technological advances we've made to date, it's natural to wonder why we are still stuck in so much emotional suffering and confusion. Your brain is the most powerful piece of "technology" you own, and you are only using a tiny fraction of it! To understand who you are and how your Past ME has led to your Current ME, we are going to broaden your understanding by getting inside your head—literally—and look at how your brilliant, beautiful brain has shaped who you are today. Having a general understanding of your mind, at least at a high level, is helpful in determining why you must go through such emotional struggles in the first place.

There are three primary forces at work which determine everything you think, say, feel, and do: your conscious mind, subconscious mind, and your unconscious mind. These three minds are constantly working together seamlessly and simultaneously to create and sustain life as you know and perceive it. In the early 1900s, Sigmund Freud popularized the image of the mind as an iceberg that sits both above and below the surface of the water. The conscious mind is your analytical mind; its job is to handle mental processes like thinking, learning, reasoning, evaluating, desiring, growing, and creating. You are in control of what you want it to do, think about, and where you want to direct its focus. The subconscious mind is the part of the iceberg that sits just below the surface of the water. It contains your beliefs, habits, and behavior patterns. The unconscious mind is that part of the iceberg that's submerged deep down below the surface where the water. The primary job of the unconscious is to control many biological functions that you can't see and, in fact, don't even think about, such as the beating of your heart, automatic breathing, digesting your food, blinking your eyes, and so much more. It also stores your memories and controls your motivation. It is important to note that the subconscious mind can't tell the difference between what is real or imagined.

POINTer

Whatever thoughts you repeatedly dream up, imagine, think about, and feel—whether they are wanted or unwanted—are etched into your subconscious mind, which ultimately become habits of thinking (your beliefs) and habits of feeling (your attitudes).

We do a whole lot of crazy things to avoid feeling any kind of emotional pain or distress. I think sometimes we give our brains a hard time. It's easy to get so frustrated, defensive, and angry when our "dumb brain" has us thinking annoying thoughts that seem to be stuck on repeat. When we sit around imagining the worst possible scenarios or outcomes or worry about situations that may never happen, we succumb to living lives riddled with fear and negativity. We struggle with memories that haunt us—getting hooked into old conversations, rehearsing what we wish we would have said or done differently—causing us to feel things like humiliation, pain, and regret every time we dig them up. Likewise, we also resent our "dumb brain" that has us opening another package of cookies, ordering another beer, and reneging on every resolution we make at the turn of a new year. Our minds can keep us stuck where we stand or march us forward to emotional freedom. Here's the good news: we do not have to be like the baby elephant, forever tied up and bound by our Past ME beliefs. There is a way to drop the rope.

Developing Emotion-Thought Bonds

As a newborn, you come into an environment consisting of your physical surroundings and the people you spend time with. Your environment plays such a significant role in shaping your beliefs and identity because in your developmental childhood years, learning is done mostly through observing and modeling the people around you. Imagine your brain is like a blank movie reel and it's recording everything it sees—everything. Your brain is intentionally designed to download and commit to memory the beliefs and behaviors of the people in your environment. Over time, you experience significant events or situations that have an impact on how you perceive your environment and yourself. The way your mind perceives these events evokes an intense emotional reaction, even if you were too young to understand what was happening in the moment. That emotion then becomes magnetized to the significant event, and they latch arms; the situation and emotion forms a bond—they now "belong" together.

Biologically, emotions are simply a chemical response to the way your brain perceives an experience. Your brain interprets billions of bits of data sent from your sensory organs, creating your reality from those interpretations. The greater the level of emotion that is evoked in an experience, the clearer you will remember it. The stronger the feeling, the stronger the memory. In fact, that's how memory is created. Your brain generates an emotion to what it's perceiving in your environment, chemicals are pumped through your body which creates a feeling (the actual sensation of the emotion), and your brain takes a snapshot of everything around you in that moment, etches it in, and stores it away for you. That significant event that caused a major emotional response is now a part of your biology; the thought is wired into your brain, and the chemical response (the emotion) is stored in your body.

POINTer

The greater the level of emotion that is evoked in an experience, the clearer you will remember it.

Your Past ME includes your experiences and memories that have been stored in your mind, heart, and body with a top layer of the emotions you associated or bonded with those memories. Your emotions, or feelings, are the icing on the cake, so to speak. There are things you don't want to remember and things you do want to remember, but it's all stored in your subconscious, waiting to be summoned and recalled at a moment's notice. Every year you spend walking the planet, encountering more and more experiences which prompt more feelings about your experiences, you become more disconnected from who you really are, and more importantly, who you believe you're capable of becoming.

When you experience any event that evokes strong emotions, it shapes the meaning around what you believe about your Current ME. Some events are especially memorable, such as the first time you felt heartache, were recognized with an award, or felt embarrassment for making a mistake. Other events are not consciously remembered at all, yet they still impact the way you react to or approach your life. So, just like the annual Thanksgiving apple pie, you repeat certain situations which evoke the attached emotion over and over throughout your life, which begins to write the movie about who you *think* you are. Now, multiply the apple pie story times a hundred other situation-emotion bonds. Now multiply it times a thousand. A million! This ongoing repetition of emotional events is called conditioning—a "set of conditions" that drive the way you think, feel, and behave.

The interesting thing is a situation doesn't have to be identical to the original one to evoke the same emotional reaction. You don't have to be baking an apple pie in the kitchen on Thanksgiving morning to be triggered by the fear of being perceived as a disappointment. When you experience an event that is similar, your nervous system will be triggered to produce the same emotional response as the initial event. Remember, your mind has automatically taken a snapshot of everything that happened physically, emotionally, and mentally, and stored it as a memory. Have you ever eaten something that made you sick, and then even many years later, the very sight or smell of that food triggers a gag reflex? Or, when you hear the song you danced to at your wedding, you immediately feel warm and fuzzy feelings of love, happiness, and joy? All these things—your environment, the significant events you've lived through, the thousands of times you've relived those events in your mind—have blended together to create the masterpiece of your Current ME.

POINTer

Your brain will predict situations to emotionally prepare you to respond the same way.

As a predicting machine, your body attaches these memories, or thoughts, with emotions and looks out for similar events that may be headed your way so it can prepare you to feel and respond the same way. It's why you can confidently think with complete certainty, "In my next relationship, I am not going to react to arguments the same way as I used to," yet when a new argument ensues, you essentially hit the replay button on your old programming. Your movie starts to look, sound, and feel like all the arguments in your past relationships despite your new, confident conviction. You accumulate scads of emotional triggers and anchors over the course of your life, and when those buttons are pushed, your brain knows exactly what movie to play because it has memorized the script. It may not seem like it now, but this is actually a good thing. You are not the sum of your patterns and triggers; that is not the real you. You are also not predestined to experience the same emotional or even physical issues or ailments that run in your family.

In the simplest of terms, observation (of anything) evokes feelings or emotions. Emotions magnetize thoughts about situations or events, and they form a bond; where one goes, so does the other. When your mind connects emotions and thoughts together, *you subconsciously give that bond a meaning*; you feel a certain way when you experience a similar event. The more times you experience the same emotion-thought bonds, the more you solidify or "fix" those bonds as real or true for your ME. Throughout your life, you have been fixing your beliefs about yourself, others, and the world around you, and therein lies the development and formation of your Current ME!

POINTer

The repetition of experiencing the same emotion-thought bonds over and over become your fixed beliefs—about yourself, others, and the world around you.

The ME That Has Been Passed Down

"There is no present or future, only the past, happening over and over again, now."

—*Eugene O'Neill, A Moon for the Misbegotten*

Many people believe their ME is largely unchangeable because of their genetic makeup. I have read that one in five people have reported that they live in emotional overwhelm, regularly medicating with antidepressants or falling victim to various addictions because of their beliefs about their genetic disposition. "Depression runs in my family" is a common fixed belief I hear from clients quite often. You can feel pretty powerless about your life when holding the belief that you are a victim of hereditary circumstances. Many of our parents helped us to form beliefs that certain health issues or illnesses are as hereditary as the "family nose." There are millions of people living their lives with assured expectation that "what happened to Mom or Dad will surely happen to me." Whether it's cancer, diabetes, heart disease, high blood pressure...the same story is being told in the mind: "I'm a product of the family genes and there's nothing I can do about it."

Both Judy and her mother struggled with perfectionism, fear of disappointment, and not being good enough, and my best guess is, so did Judy's grandmother, great-grandmother, and so on down the generational line. It wouldn't surprise me a bit that starting in her childhood, Judy's mother went to desperate measures to be pleasing and perfect for her mother, suffering a lifetime of perfectionistic anxiety along the way. According to traditional genetic thinking, Judy should expect to inherit the same traits and characteristics— "like mother like daughter." Fortunately, according to a rather new science called epigenetics, it has been proven that the genes found in your DNA do not actually have the power to "decide" your physical biology. Without getting knee deep into the scientific weeds, epigenetic research has found that some of the world's most common diseases are in fact not handed down because of our genetic makeup; rather, *genes can switch on or off because of our beliefs and the way we perceive our environment.*

Let's apply this concept to the movie of your life. Imagine the actors in your movie (your cast, so to speak) are played by your human cells. Your genetic makeup, or DNA, is the script, which contains the actors' lines, determining how they perform their roles. The overall concept of traditional genetics would be like screenwriting—simply writing the storyline. The concept of epigenetics, on the other hand, is more like directing. Your movie script might be the same as your mother's or father's but as the director, you can choose to change certain scenes, altering the movie to your liking. Looking through the lens of epigenetics, the way you perceive your environment creates a chemical modification to your genes. Certain genes that are associated with diseases like cancer or Alzheimer's, for example, can be switched on or off simply by changing your environment and beliefs.

How incredible is it to know that your genes don't really control your life!? When you choose to see your life through a happy, healthy, hopeful lens instead of shameful or fearful one, you can change your entire movie.

Changing Your Movie

We've all created a unique movie about our Current and Ideal MEs—who we are, how we perceive the world around us, what we believe we're capable of achieving in life—yet we are all but oblivious to the fact that we have the ability to change our movie at any time. We constantly mistake our limited perceptions as reality, and as a result, it can cause us immense turmoil and confusion. Most people live their entire lives accepting a ME that's predicated on labels and illusions. We are so determined to stick to *who we believe we are* that we accept what we think we know about ourselves as the truth. When you limit your Ideal ME to your past experiences, your beliefs become "fixed"—*you become the baby elephant.* In order to change your movie, including the beliefs that helped you write it in the first place, you must begin to explore the desires and capabilities of your Ideal ME so you can elevate your life to a whole new level.

POINTer

Your ME has been molded from your experiences, yes. But it's the emotion that is attached to the experience that is holding you back.

Let's rewind Judy's movie. Imagine Judy pulling the apple pie out of the oven that first Thanksgiving morning; the apples were too firm, she used too much cinnamon, and the edges of the crust were burnt to a charcoal crisp. And rather than labeling the pie a disappointment or a failure, her mother labeled it "a unique masterpiece, perfectly imperfect." What if the botched pie created a lighthearted rumble of laughter instead of a dark cloud of disappointment? Instead of living under a dark cloud of not being good enough throughout her life, Judy might've embodied a healthy sense of humor, flexibility, and self-acceptance.

Just like the baby elephant tied to the tree, we learn to adapt to and live with our surroundings and fixed beliefs, no matter how they feel. We also have the power to explore new possibilities we never considered before. You may feel emotionally tied up and held back in certain areas of your life, but the ropes can be broken. The labels and judgments you've accepted over the course of your life can be released if you want to live a life of freedom. It's just a matter of choice, and now is your time to choose. You can hack the system, tap into your subconscious, and transform your Current ME into your Ideal ME.

Hacking the System

> *"Everything that happens in your mind has a physical representation in your brain, and everything that happens in your brain correlates with what happens in your body."*
>
> —Deepak Chopra

Your subconscious mind is like a supercomputer that sorts through an endless amount of data and stores it all up to protect you. Your conscious mind represents the applications or programs you can choose to load onto the computer based on what functions you want it to perform. Your subconscious mind is more like the operating system those programs sit on—it simply runs the programs, automatically, that have been installed. If there are no new instructions for it to follow, it will boot up the same way tomorrow as it did yesterday; therefore, you continue to create a future that is really set in the past.

So, how was your operating system designed in the first place? It's as easy as Thanksgiving apple pie. Your subconscious programming is established because of your environment (modeling others as a young child and taking beliefs and labels of those closest to you), the significant emotional events you've experienced (your emotion-thought bonds), and repetitive conditioning (your habits and patterns).

POINTer

Your subconscious mind can only perform the functions that have been programmed.

It's not possible to use the *conscious mind* to stop or erase the programs that are running on autopilot in the subconscious. Your subconscious mind can only perform the functions that have been programmed. Imagine for a moment that your computer starts "misbehaving"—random windows begin to pop up, tabs unexpectedly close, and programs shut down. If you yell at the computer, "Stop misbehaving!" it's not going to stop what it's doing. To experience transformation, you must access the operating system (your subconscious mind). The good news is, it *is* possible to move from sitting on top of the iceberg to wading in the shallow waters of your subconscious mind where emotional transformation can begin. To do this, you need to change your brainwaves.

Riding the Waves

"Energy is the language spoken by your body."   —*Ilchi Lee*

Neural oscillations, or brainwaves, have been researched and observed since the early 1920s, starting with German psychiatrist Hans Berger, who's best-known for inventing electroencephalography (EEG). These brainwaves are electrical impulses that range from fast to slow and are measured in hertz (Hz), or cycles per second, and each band has a unique purpose. The way you experience your movie is vastly different depending on which brainwave band you are functioning in. Depending on which wave you happen to be riding at the time, your brain will function in different ways to support you.

Gamma

The fastest band is called gamma, and that's the wave you're riding when you require intense concentration or solve complex problems. Gamma can be induced through meditation, generally by those highly trained like Tibetan monks. In this state, deep clarity and awareness, as well as compassion and even bliss have been reported.

Beta

The next fastest is beta, where most of us spend the bulk of our time. Beta is your everyday conscious and alert state. In beta, your attention is focused on the external world where your brain is aroused, busily interpreting the signals that your sensory organs are sending, drowning in the chemical cocktail of emotion that the brain is pumping, often producing anxiety, stress, and unease.

Alpha

Alpha waves are slower than beta, allowing your body to become more relaxed. Think of alpha as "being in the zone"—it's great for thinking about memories and activating your imagination and engaging in visualization.

Theta

Dropping below alpha is theta, where you become deeply relaxed. Theta feels like a dreamlike state of reverie where you are still awake, but close to being asleep. In theta, your focus and attention are directed inward rather than on the things that are happening in the world around you.

Delta

The slowest band is called delta, when you are asleep or in deep transcendental meditation. Theta and delta waves are linked to the subconscious mind, enabling "easier access" to universal, collective consciousness, also referred to as all-knowing intelligence, or spirit.

By changing your brainwaves, you can shift from being mentally productive to rising to peak intellectual focus and alertness, or from being creative and engaging your imagination to unwinding at the end of the day and preparing for a restful sleep. Because most of the time you are either asleep (delta) or in an alert, conscious state (beta), you likely associate your Current ME with the version of you that's wandering around in beta. You need to operate in this frequency to function in everyday life. It helps you access things like logic, reason, and discernment. You want to have clear judgment to cross the road or discuss an important work matter with your boss, right? In beta, you are very active in your conscious mind, continually thinking, reasoning, and analyzing. When you can drop into the relaxed brain state of theta, those conscious survival mechanisms can rest. You are relaxed enough to enter your internal world and tap into your inner intelligence.

You know that dreamy moment just before you wake up or before you fall asleep? This "twilight zone" of consciousness is the gateway to the subconscious, where you can access the old memories and patterns that have been an integral part of the development of your Current ME. From the ages of two to six, children spend most of their time in theta, and it's in this state that the subconscious is primarily programmed. Everything you witnessed as a child, including the beliefs of the people around you, became a part of your ME. In theta you're able to communicate with this inner intelligence (your subconscious) and gain insight into the beliefs and emotions stored within your body. Theta is the wave you (or your client) will ride to access the subconscious mind and transform the emotional patterns that are causing distress.

It's a Matter of the Heart

> *"Follow your heart but take your brain with you."*
> —*Alfred Adler*

In theta frequency, your brain and heart have coherence, meaning their waves are in sync. Throughout the ages, the heart has always been considered a source of a deeper knowing. The ancient Egyptians believed the heart was in fact the source of wisdom, not the brain. You've probably been told more than once to "listen to your heart" or asked, "Are you thinking with your head or your heart?" Your brain and heart are certainly connected, and what's interesting to know is that 10% of your nerve fibers send information from the brain down to the heart, whereas 90% of them ascend from the heart to your brain. While, scientifically, a lot that remains a mystery, this information coming from the heart has been shown to interact with and affect your emotional centers, as well as your higher cognition centers. So, the heart is not just an organ that pumps blood; it plays a massive role in your emotions and how you make decisions.

Our hearts are so powerful! The magnetic field it produces has been said to be 5,000 times stronger than the magnetic field produced by the brain. So, what does that mean for you? Biologically speaking, when you tap into your heart, the fear mechanisms in your brain begin to "quiet down." When you access your theta frequency band and connect your brain with your heart, you enter the sweet spot, or the zone, opening to and allowing for direct communication with your subconscious and the all-knowing intelligence of universal energy.

POINTer

The beliefs you hold about yourself are fueled by emotions that are full of energy. What you feel sends energy out into the world around you.

Everything in the universe emits an energetic vibrational frequency, including you and your emotions! Science proves that emotions create magnetic, energetic fields that can be measured. Emotional frequencies directly impact your body's energy fields, and the effects can be seen, felt, and measured. Emotions are constantly firing through your body like sudden sparks of electricity, igniting and activating all that you do, think, see, and dream. You experience them in the form of "feel"ings, and they affect your attitude, self-esteem, and the beliefs you hold about yourself.

Emotions are information and a communication system that exist for our highest good. They serve us with their intentions to inform us on so many different levels. The perceived fears, blockages, beliefs, memories, and emotions you believe are holding you back or causing you pain are also providing you with a benefit, and they always have. As you'll soon learn through the P.O.I.N.T. method, there is a gift, or what I like to call an "upside" to every emotional pattern that's waiting to be discovered!

There is ALWAYS an upside!

Seeing Your ME in a Whole New Light

"Always remember, your focus determines your reality."
—*George Lucas*

Throughout the book so far, you've been seeing the journey of your life as a movie that has actors, plots, scenes, screenwriters, directors, and producers that all play an integral part, whether it's a romantic comedy, an action-packed blockbuster, or a melodrama. As humans, we are all making our own movie, and no one movie is the same as another. Your experiences and expectations are constantly creating your perception of your Current ME from the inside out because of the beliefs you hold and *where you put your focus.*

In making her first apple pie, Judy had filtered out the compliments her mother had given her. She didn't notice the way her mother looked at her with pride and approval when she cut the apples and rolled the pie dough for the first time. Judy's mother's pride and approval were indeed there, but her focus was on the emotions that arose when the pie came out of the oven, imperfect. Disappointment. Failure. Not good enough. Do you see how Judy made observations about her environment that resulted in her beliefs about her ME?

Today, from the outside looking in, most people would agree that Judy was living a pretty darn good life. She presented herself beautifully. Her hair, nails, and wardrobe were, by most standards, well...perfect! Her home was spotless, her social calendar was full, she excelled in her career, and was on the verge of landing a very senior-level, high-paying position. People often commented on her fastidiousness—highly organized with an attention to detail that was second to none. She was the standard-bearer for herself and her entire team. All these attributes contributed to Judy's team's achievements and healthy commissions each quarter. So, why was Judy still so emotionally challenged?

For Judy, the downside effects of perfectionism were crystal clear, but the upside had been *filtered out of her focus*. She complained of feeling permanently exhausted from the insomnia that had plagued her for years. When she described her work life, she said, "I always seem to bite off more than I can chew," which inevitably caused mounting anxiety with each new responsibility she took on. While her co-workers and teammates praised her level of detail, from her perspective, she could only experience her perfectionism as "draining and debilitating" to consistently keep up the standard. She also described having feelings of stress, loneliness, and detachment. There would always be another level of expectation and perfection she would have to live up to, and she had reached her breaking point. In Judy's mind, perfectionism was delivering nothing but pain because that was her focus.

"When you change the way you look at things, the things you look at change." —*Dr. Wayne W. Dyer*

Remember, the emotion-thought bonds we experienced in our past were either processed effectively or they weren't. The beliefs we've held about the characters in our movie have been writing the script of our subconscious mind for a very long time. As we replay our movie repeatedly, telling ourselves and others the same stories, we cement those emotion-thought bonds until they feel impenetrable. When we've seen a movie a hundred times, we develop the ability to recite the lines by heart. We can anticipate what's going to happen next, how it will look, sound, and feel. It's the very reason you see people attracting the same types of people into their lives, reliving the same types of relationships and scenarios. You may have hired a "stand-in" to play the previous actor's part, but the movie remains the same. The automatically programmed emotions you most frequently focus on will take center stage, no matter if you choose the hero or the villain. The truth of your Current ME is only the truth as your Past ME *has chosen* to believe it, but the fact is, it isn't really the truth at all. Your Current ME is playing out the script which was written from an interpretation from your early childhood. You simply grew up.

By now, you're probably wondering how much longer your Current ME must continue to fight through the limiting beliefs created by your Past ME to reach the transformation into your Ideal ME.

We're almost there…let me point the way.

PART II

P.O.I.N.T.ing the Way to Emotional Transformation

PART II

P.O.I.N.T.ing
the Way to Emotional Transformation

"The butterfly said to the sun, 'They can't stop talking about my transformation. I can only do it once in my lifetime. If only they knew they can do it at any time and in countless ways.'"

—*Dodinsky*

It's Time to Fly

Just like the caterpillar, we are all born to pursue growth and self-actualization—to become the truth of who we were created to be. We all possess an innate desire to become our actualized potential, our Ideal ME, to discover who we really are, seeking our true identity and ultimate purpose in life. The caterpillar naturally moves toward its ultimate destiny; it transforms into the butterfly through a metamorphic process, and that process takes time and patience. You'll remember from the very beginning of this book that the FreedomPOINT method isn't about "changing" old behaviors to new ones; it's about experiencing complete transformation. The caterpillar doesn't change into a butterfly, *it already is the butterfly*. They are the same organism and have the exact same DNA; they are just at different developmental stages. The cells containing the blueprint for the butterfly were always inside. To reach its ideal state and evolve to its highest potential, the caterpillar must follow its inner intelligence that its destiny is not to crawl—it's to fly. In the same way, the blueprint for our Ideal ME has always lived inside of us, too.

We are walking miracles, magnificent in our design; we have simply programmed ourselves in ways that haven't yielded our most desired outcomes. As a result, we become like the baby elephant, restrained and resigned to living a life that's oblivious to our full potential. There is still so much that is unknown about the brain: accessing higher consciousness, optimizing altered brainwave states, and strengthening our mind-body and heart-brain connections. What's so wonderful is that it's not necessary for us to fully understand the capacity of our inner intelligence in order to transform and break free from our past neural wiring and programming.

The old paradigm doesn't work anymore!

Just as many once believed Earth was flat, when they learned it was actually the center of the solar system, they were forced to admit they got it wrong. They were just looking at things from the wrong perspective, so chalk it up to a misunderstanding. Perceiving emotions as good or bad is also a misunderstanding; I call it The Great Misunderstanding. We have completely missed the fact we have an internal guidance system that communicates *through* emotion. We have assumed that emotions that feel bad *are* bad. We've therefore ignored any of the direction and benefits they intended. Think of it like having a GPS system and then refusing to consult it. It is there but unused. We've also misunderstood our ability to transform our patterns. Yes, we can all become the butterfly. When we are willing to stop judging our behaviors, beliefs, and habitual patterns of thinking and feeling, we can work with the genius of the communication system we've been given. When we can look objectively at what's there, why it's there, and what the original intention of it was, we can begin to understand the genius within ourselves. We can embrace every emotion as a resource to guide and help us evolve and grow into our Ideal ME.

It's time for a paradigm shift.

Here's where I'm going to ask you to consider a new possibility. What if every one of your beliefs, behaviors, and emotion patterns you judge so harshly have always shown up in support of your well-being? Would you look at them differently? Would you treat them differently?

We must have admiration and awe for the body and the brain; they are more complex than we will ever understand, and they are always working first and foremost to ensure our survival. Though many of your Past and Current ME beliefs may be causing you stress and anxiety, they continue to stick around because they still have a job to do. The crazy thing is, they're still trying to do the same job they were created for (oftentimes many decades ago) and are operating as if you're still the young child they came to protect. The emotion programs running your life are not always (in fact, rarely) of your own choosing. Technically, they're not your fault, and they're certainly not your destiny. Once survival is no longer an issue, the body and the brain work to support growth and the realization of our full potential.

Your subconscious mind is always looking out for you. While the subconscious mind doesn't know the difference between what's real or imagined, this can be both a shortcoming and an advantage. Its greatest mission is to protect and help you thrive. Your conscious mind is always trying to make sense of your behaviors and rarely understands the original intentions of the protection patterns the subconscious has put in place. Since it doesn't understand, it creates judgments, and seriously, makes stuff up. Let's say, for example, you grew up in a situation where trusting the wrong person could have been a threat to your safety or even your survival. The belief you formed was "keep people at a distance because it's not safe to trust them." The long-term downside of this belief could have you living life in isolation or struggling to build and maintain healthy, trusting relationships. But rest assured, this belief stuck around for a reason. It came as a protection mechanism to heighten your awareness. You probably developed a kind of sixth sense about people with ill intentions.

Not every limiting pattern you run is based on a traumatic experience. Getting a "C" on your report card can set in motion a lifetime of intense study habits. So, keep in mind, patterns with less emotional charge or element of fear around them can be just as impactful long term. Take indecision as an example. It's a pattern usually based on the fear of making a mistake, getting something wrong. This may not result in huge pain, and it does have an upside to it. If you don't make a decision, then you can't make a "wrong" one. You may have become accustomed to accepting this as "who you are" or "how you operate" yet you may not be 100% satisfied with the results you're getting. You may have sometimes wondered why this is the case or what it would be like if something changed in that space. The good news is there is an opportunity to have a "tune-up" in such circumstances, where even a small shift can result in major positive consequences long term. It's never *au fait accompli*. Indeed, you may be happy with your life, or your client may tell you the same, but know there is always room to grow and progress your life at an accelerated pace if you want it.

I reiterate, the difficult, challenging, and even painful emotions we experience are indeed benefitting us in some way. As we embrace this new paradigm, the fear and judgment of our emotional patterns dissipate, and we can honor them and transform them.

It's time for transformation.

At some point in your life, you've probably seen a movie that had more than one ending as an option. It is a common practice for screenwriters to produce alternative endings to create different resolutions to the same story. How the movie ends can mean the difference between the movie becoming a blockbuster or a box-office flop. When you are living as your Ideal ME, you allow your true, divine nature to write an alternative ending to your movie. The beliefs and patterns of your Past and Current MEs can be rewritten! And through the P.O.I.N.T. method, your Ideal ME will show you clearly how to write the ending you want; one that replaces sadness with joy, depression with vibrancy, insecurity with self-confidence, shame with deservingness, or fear with courage. When your Ideal ME teams up with the information of your subconscious mind and higher intelligence of the universe, there is no limit to your creative possibilities.

Your Ideal ME is the person who emerges when, one by one, the limiting emotional constructs are peeled back like an onion, confronted, understood, and then reprogrammed and reconditioned with a new, more supportive strategy. The caterpillar must first surrender to becoming the chrysalis inside the cocoon before it can transform into the butterfly. In the process of releasing the past and preparing for the future, the caterpillar digests itself, except for a special group of cells called "imaginal cells." As the name implies, the imaginal cells contain a future potential—a magnificent, winged creature, free from its past bindings and free to fly. Within you is the intelligence to imagine and live your highest potential. You can rewrite your script in countless ways, over and over.

Through the P.O.I.N.T. method, you can transform your life and begin to fly.

You are about to learn how to turn emotional struggles into strengths, to transform beyond the emotional bonds and patterns that have held you back so you can enjoy a life of freedom that lasts. This method will help you discover an impeccable realm of information—a system of communication that goes beyond anything you've ever imagined. It is my sincere desire that you will learn from it, work with it, and create the emotional transformation results you want for yourself and/ or your clients. There is no magic wand here, but the results are indeed magical. When you allow yourself to access the infinite intelligence that lives within your Ideal ME, you will discover that YOU are the magic.

Now, let's learn how to process emotions effectively and unlock the door to releasing all that's untrue about your Current ME and allow your Ideal ME to emerge in all its glory!

Tips for Facilitators/Practitioners

I love using acronyms to help me remember key bits of information. The P.O.I.N.T. acronym helps you easily follow the formula for transformation: Prepare, Observe, Inquire, Negotiate, and Transform.

The NO RISK pre-frame is designed to help you understand and explain some of the fundamental differences in the FreedomPOINT coaching method. This helps dispel any reservations or trepidations about the FreedomPOINT experience. NO RISK stands for Non-intrusive, Only about emotions, Rapport building, Intelligent, Service-oriented, and Knowledge.

Non-intrusive

Unlike some therapeutic models, the P.O.I.N.T. method is not designed to "dig up" painful emotional trauma. The conversation with the subconscious mind is gentle and supportive, allowing you to retrieve information easily and painlessly.

Only about emotions

It is important to disengage from lengthy, intimate details of the stories and events that have caused emotional distress and focus primarily on the information communicated about "how that made you feel."

Rapport

As a certified practitioner, it is imperative to develop rapport and trust, being intentional to create a genuine connection with your client. Take some time in the beginning to learn about their circumstances, asking what's important to them, and acknowledging whatever they're feeling is real and key to their success.

Intelligent emotion

Perhaps the most important premise of all is that every emotion is intelligent, intentional, and contains valuable information. Every emotion is always intended for the client's well-being and best interests. As they go through the process, the client will be able to identify where they feel the emotions in the body.

Service-oriented

All emotions are in service to our basic human needs on some level, even when it doesn't feel like it. Just as every system in the body is working to support and sustain us in life, so is our emotional system.

Knowledge

Remain open and curious to the knowledge and wisdom that exists within you and is communicated through the subconscious mind. Trust the information you receive.

Now, on to the star of the show—the whole purpose in writing this book: the P.O.I.N.T. method.

What's the POINT?

In developing the P.O.I.N.T. method, there were two questions always at the top of my mind: "How can we create real transformation in every coaching conversation?" and "How can we get into the proverbial "ZONE?" You know...the zone of genius, of ease, of our authentic gifts and strengths—the zone of accelerated and amplified performance. So, I looked at numerous models, modalities, and techniques to see what they had in common, what was unique or slightly different about each of them, what elements I loved, and what, if anything, seemed to be missing. Then I tested different combinations with the insights that had already been revealed to me. What eventuated is FreedomPOINT. Freedom, because we all crave the freedom to be ourselves, to be loved and accepted unconditionally for who we were born to be. POINT because it's the acronym that describes the process to get ourselves and our clients to that emotional freedom.

And you ask, "What's the POINT?"

P.O.I.N.T. represents the five essential elements to this method and provides the framework to follow as you guide your clients to transformation.

Step 1: Prepare – Prepare yourself and your client for a successful session.

Step 2: Observe – Observe the patterns creating stress, distress, or holding the client back.

Step 3: Inquire – Guide the client into a light, meditative state. Ask a series of specific questions to identify the location of the information and reveal the intentions, benefits, and challenges of the program(s).

Step 4: Negotiate – Negotiate with the subconscious to create a new pattern that will preserve the upside and eliminate the downside.

Step 5: Transform – Transform the pattern by releasing it, upgrading it, combining with a new resource, or installing a brand-new pattern. Project into the future.

Freedom POINT

STEP 1: PREPARE

Preparing Yourself

The first step in the P.O.I.N.T. method is to prepare yourself for a successful session. You begin by centering and grounding yourself, creating a calm, quiet, environment that's free of distractions. This may sound like an easy task but being in the present moment with yourself or a client and staying in this state for a prolonged period takes practice. It's natural for your mind to wander. It wants to think back to the phone call you had with your friend yesterday or plan what's for dinner tonight. You can also bet on it to do its best to silently narrate what's happening in the present moment or ask inane questions that lead you down some uncharted rabbit hole. You can think of this silent chatter as your mind's default mode, and it's your responsibility to change the setting before engaging in the process.

When your mind is fully present, there is a gap that is created in the mental thought process. This gap causes the silent chatter of the mind to dissipate, then stillness and peace is invited to take its place. This is the gift, or "present" of true presence. By quieting your mind and becoming more present, you will feel more alive, alert, and relaxed. You are now free to be 100% present, as if nothing else exists beyond your desire to serve the person you're working with. This is an essential first step to establish the proper energetic space for your session.

To create a state of presence in the preparation step, I have another acronym for you as a prompt: FACE. It is your reminder to Focus, Affirm, Center, and Engage.

Focus

Close your eyes, relax your body, and imagine any distractions disappearing. You can direct your focus by repeating the statement "I am here now; I am ready to serve."

Affirm

Set your intention to serve only the highest good. Expectations of outcomes are dangerous; as with every session, you cannot predict what or how the subconscious mind will choose to communicate. As a coach and facilitator, your purpose is to discover and guide the conversation without bias and for the client's greatest level of wellbeing.

Center

Centering means creating alignment and awareness of your Emotional Center (your heart), your Physical Center (your gut), your Mental Center (your thinking mind), and your Spiritual Center (your intuition). You can do this by doing a short meditation, taking some cleansing breaths into your heart space, or recite a brief mantra or prayer.

Engage

Engage and expand your sensory acuity, which is simply your level of paying attention. In any coaching session, you want to intentionally raise your level of awareness to what's going on around you. In this case, your awareness is directed specifically toward the client. As a coach and facilitator, your primary responsibility is to observe and respond. With heightened acuity, you will not only hear the information the subconscious is presenting through the client, but you will also notice many clues. You'll pick up the nuances of body language, facial expressions, emotional reactions, tears, sounds, and postures. And often, you'll receive messages—I call them communication downloads that somehow come through your own intuition. Never overlook the importance or impact of effective preparation. Give yourself and your client the grace you both deserve; take a few minutes to invite your senses to wake up, pay attention, and make astute observations.

Preparing the Client

Once you've prepared yourself, you want to prepare the client and set them up for success. Just as you took the time to quiet your own mind and get centered, it's equally important to allow the client to "land" in the energetic space you've created for the session. Be cognizant of where their head may be. Are they nervous? Have they had a stressful day? Or are they coming to the session with a level of uncertainty or anxiety? As the session begins, in person or virtually, you want to "equalize and merge" the energy. Greet them by using a gentle tone of voice and speak a little slower than usual to calm any excited or nervous energy they may have. You'll learn what a powerful role your voice will play throughout the coaching session.

With your client's permission, I do encourage you or your client to record your sessions for the purpose of reviewing and revisiting anytime in the future.

FreedomPOINT

STEP 2: OBSERVE

Step 2 of P.O.I.N.T. is all about discovering what circumstances are creating stress in their lives, then probing with the question, "How does that make you feel?" What thoughts, beliefs, and behaviors accompany these emotions? This allows you to observe and objectively capture the presenting patterns.

Asking Questions and Listening for Clues

As the facilitator, you are looking for clues, and finding those clues is more readily accomplished by knowing what to ask, look, and listen and listen for. Emotional patterns show up in a variety of ways, so in this step, you'll need to be prepared with some probing questions in the event the client experiences a blockage or shutdown. You can use these questions to spark the conversation and be sure to listen for clues that come from the client's responses. As a coach, developing acute and intentional listening skills takes practice and begins with setting the intention to do so. Employing active listening is key to helping the client discover and pinpoint the emotion programs currently running.

POINTers to help guide you in what to ask and listen for: (Use these with yourself as well.)

"What creates undue stress in your life?"

"What do you believe is achievable for you?"

"What question(s) do you perpetually ask yourself?"

"What are your beliefs about life, love, success, money?"

"Which of your emotions are easily and frequently triggered?" (e.g.: anger, frustration, impatience)

"What's getting in the way of the results you want to achieve?"

"When you make a mistake, what do you say to yourself?"

"What do you say, do, or feel when things don't go as expected?"

"When others let you down, what do you say to yourself? To others? About them?"

The "cherry on top" follow-up question to ask after every other question: *"How does that make you feel?"*

Once you know how they feel, you can put a name to what they are experiencing. Naming the emotions helps you become crystal clear on what specific patterns are at play, and there are typically more than one. As a beginner coach/facilitator, you want to start small. Take on no more than 1-3 emotion patterns in any given session to avoid overloading yourself with too many elements to focus on. As your expertise grows, your capacity to address more patterns will expand quickly.

Keep in mind, emotion patterns are not good or bad; they are simply energy and information designed to protect, guide, and motivate us toward a particular outcome. Their intention is to help and never to harm. As the facilitator, your goal is to focus solely on the information that's communicated through these patterns and forego any predetermined judgments. Your role is to remain neutral and completely objective as you guide your client through the conversation with the subconscious.

As you navigate this conversation, be careful not to get caught up in the details of the circumstances or stories. As an issue is addressed, *only* listen for the emotions, language patterns, and beliefs associated with the issue. These are the things you'll be exploring throughout the session. Remember, the power question that reveals underlying beliefs and emotion patterns is: "How does that make you feel?"

POINTer

Emotion patterns are not good or bad. They are signals. They exist to protect, direct, or motivate us toward a particular outcome, and their intention is always for our good and not to be harmful in any way. They are communication—energy and information that is here to serve.

Uncovering Bucket Emotions

Sometimes it can take a bit more probing to get past "bucket emotions" such as hurt, pain, stress, or fear to get beneath the surface and find out what's really going on. Here's an example to explain what I mean by bucket emotions: a client (let's call her Maggie) comes to her session saying, "The stress at work is coming back; I thought we dealt with that already?" I explained to Maggie that "stress" is a big bucket into which we throw many emotions, like overwhelm, worry, anxiousness, pressure, and countless other stress-producers.

I questioned, *"What are the feelings creating this added stress? How do you really feel at work or about your work?"* Maggie went on to share that she felt disrespected, unappreciated, overlooked, undervalued, humiliated, embarrassed, and like she didn't fit in, and no one had her back. As you can see, there was a lot of "stuff" in the stress bucket, and we needed to find out what it was to help her with the transformation that would handle all of it. At the crux of the issue was "feeling disrespected," and we discovered in her session that "self-respect" was the antidote to neutralize it all.

While moving through the Observe step of the process, it's important to recognize that patterns rarely work in isolation. More often than not, there are many emotion patterns that can be linked to one core emotion or belief. So, keep probing for those clues! Remember, you're the guide and you want to create a reassuring environment so the client can readily express their emotions and not resist them. With your help, they will learn to embrace and understand the power and intention of all their so-called "negative" emotions.

Another example is a client who shared a story about a partner who cheated on him. The core emotion was jealousy; however, the client also held a belief, a personal judgment about jealousy—that "being jealous" is a sign of weakness and insecurity. So, the overriding emotion was the need for control. His protection strategy became one of disconnection rather than to experience feeling weak or ashamed. Our jealous client discovered that jealousy does not equal weakness, and its real intention is to show him what is important to him and what he really wants.

Measuring Emotional Frequency and Intensity

As you observe in Step 2, you also want to establish the frequency and intensity of each emotion. It's important not to make any personal assumptions or judgments about what the client is experiencing.

Frequency and intensity will vary widely from one client to the next, and even one emotion to the next. It's logical to conclude that emotion patterns of high intensity and constancy are the ones to address first, and yet, this is not always the case. In the next step, you'll learn how the body guides the order in which patterns need to be addressed.

It's also important to understand that even emotions at low levels of intensity and frequency can have extreme downsides long term. Because of this, the subconscious may guide you to start with patterns that may appear to be insignificant, which is why you must suspend assumptions, expectations, and judgments about any beliefs, feelings, or behaviors. Trust the wisdom of the subconscious to guide you exactly where you need to go.

Once you've identified a few of the emotion patterns you're going to explore, you want to assess the intensity and frequency of these feelings. Here's a simple graph to help the client quantify their experience.

EMOTION: FREQUENCY & INTENSITY

Frequency

On a scale of 1-10 (1 being 10% or less and 10 being 100% of the time), how frequently do you experience the emotion(s)?

| 1 | 2 | 3 | 4 | 5 | 6 | 7 | 8 | 9 | 10 |

Intensity

On a scale of 1-10 (1 being the least intense and 10 being the most intense), on average, what is the intensity level of the emotion(s)?

| 1 | 2 | 3 | 4 | 5 | 6 | 7 | 8 | 9 | 10 |

<u>Frequency Questions to Ask</u>:

>*"On a scale of one to ten, with ten being 100% of the time, how frequently is this emotion present?"*

>*"And in what ways, if any, do these feelings interfere with your life?"*

<u>Intensity Questions to Ask</u>:

>*"From one to ten, with ten being extremely intense, on average, what is the intensity level of these emotions?"*

>*"And what impact, if any, does this have on you, your life, and the people around you?"*

Identifying the Downside

Next, you want the client to express what they perceive as the downside to each emotion.

<u>POINTers to help guide the client in expressing the downside:</u>

>*"What are the consequences of these feelings, thoughts, and beliefs?"*

>*"What are they costing you now?"*

>*"What have they cost you in the past?"*

>*"What will they cost you in the future if you don't address them now?"*

>*"What areas of your life are most impacted by this emotion/ pattern?"*

>*"How are these feelings limiting your progress or success now?"*

>*"What will you miss out on in the future because of these emotions/patterns?"*

"What could you gain without this feeling?"

"What would life be like without these feelings, beliefs, thoughts, and behaviors?"

"If we could transform these limiting feelings into ones of personal empowerment, what would that be worth to you?"

We never want to diminish or negate someone's perspective of what happened and how they feel about it. What we want to do is help them identify their strength, power, and ability regardless of anything they've been through. Your job as a coach is to be mindful and to listen without judgment, with curiosity, always seeking to help your client understand why these patterns are in place. There is an upside to the original intention behind every emotional habit.

FreedomPOINT

STEP 3: INQUIRE

"The art and science of asking questions is the source of all knowledge."   —*Adolf Berle*

In Step 3, the conscious mind is given permission to take a step back so the subconscious mind can step forward. In the previous step, you identified the client's limiting patterns through careful questioning and observation. Now you are ready to continue the conversation directly with the subconscious. Here we locate the patterns (inside or outside the body), determine which pattern we work on first, find out its original intention, and then explore both the upside (benefits) and the downside (limitations) of the pattern's strategy. The key to Inquire is to ask questions of the pattern *as if it was a person.*

Transitioning from Beta to Theta

Our goal is to shift the client from beta brainwave frequency to theta, enabling them to shut down the highly active "monkey mind" and tap into their subconscious mind. Theta is the frequency band that opens the doorway to emotional transformation. The theta frequency band feels still, peaceful, and effortless. Activating this frequency opens a portal to hidden information and intuitive wisdom that's not accessible in beta. In theta, one becomes an objective observer of their mind, no longer feeling trapped inside of the chaotic limitations of beta. In other words, the monkey can put down the drum. The client is carefully guided into a light meditative trance, but unlike in hypnotherapy, they are fully aware of what is happening and will remember most of the insights that come through.

Demystifying Trance

In guiding clients into theta, it's important to keep in mind that most people are uncomfortable feeling "out of control." There is a distinct difference between being in a trance state and being hypnotized. It's natural for clients to have questions as to what they're about to experience, so before you begin, establish trust by easing any fears or misconceptions and describing what to expect. You can use the following reassuring statements:

"In the theta (light-trance) state:

you will feel very relaxed, centered, and safe. You will be somewhat conscious of what's being communicated, but your focus will be directed inward.

you will not be hypnotized. You will always be in control and in charge of your communication and decisions.

you will only respond to questions and accept suggestions that are consistent and in alignment with your own internal values and beliefs."

In the FreedomPOINT method there is a specific script we use to facilitate this state, which is downloadable for free at go.getfpc.com/gifts.

Begin inducing relaxation by instructing them to inhale deeply through the nose and exhale slowly and gently through the mouth. Ask the client to close their eyes, shutting out any external distractions and pulling their full awareness inward. Instruct them to keep their eyes closed throughout the entire process to maintain their inner presence. As their breathing slows, you want them to notice the sensations that arise in their body. Speak to the movement that accompanies the breath, such as the belly expanding like a balloon with the inhale, the rib cage opening, the lungs filling up with air, and the chest expanding while the shoulders shift back slightly.

"Notice the sensations in your body, and the more you notice, the more aware you become. And the more aware you become, the more you notice, as you go deeper and deeper into connection with the physical body."

POINTer

Using phrases such as "as you go deeper and deeper" is an intentional technique, using autosuggestion to help the client's body literally follow the instruction or suggestion you're giving them through verbal cues. This also prompts them to drop into a more relaxed, open, and aware state.

As the client becomes more relaxed, ask them to *"Breathe as though you're breathing directly into your heart, and soon, you'll become aware of your heartbeat."*

This prompts them to notice what will be occurring next. After they've taken a few breaths into their heart, follow by saying, *"When you begin to notice, sense, feel, or hear your heartbeat, just say 'Yes.'—Thaaaatttt's right."*

At this point, they should be in a lucid, light, trance-like state, and you're ready to inquire with the subconscious by asking a series of highly effective questions. The first question is used to determine where the pattern is located inside or outside the body.

Mapping the Patterns

Ask: *"Where, if anywhere, inside or outside the body, is information called _____ (emotion)?"*

Notice that in the question being asked here, the emotion is referred to as "information." This is because information does not have a connotation as good or bad; it's completely neutral.

POINTer

Using the phrase "Where, if anywhere" eliminates all responsibility from the client to produce a "right" answer. It also eliminates any of the facilitator's assumptions as to where this information might be presenting. It gives the client the opportunity to say, "I don't feel it" without being wrong. If the information isn't here, simply move on. It's possible it can't be located because we have called it by the wrong name.

As the body is scanned for information, the client is typically able to identify an area of the body where the information presents itself fairly quickly, if not immediately. There is no right or wrong response; the information can reveal itself virtually anywhere. In fact, the client may disclose that the information is standing right beside them like a shadow, or perhaps they feel a sort of pressure that's pushing them from behind.

This is what I use to map the location of the information given. It helps me track the patterns and direct the questions to the right locations and the information that's present there. It also tells me where to go back and check for the presence of the patterns. This is a highly useful tool to help solidify your learnings and gain confidence in your ability to master the process.

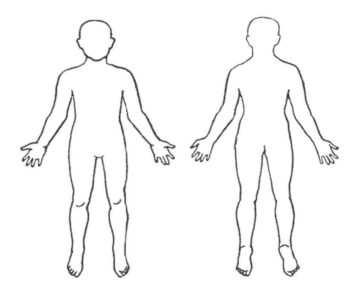

Body Scan Example

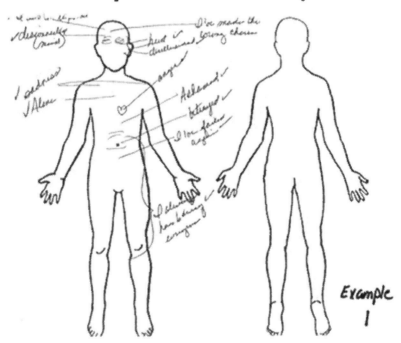

Example 1

Metaphors

Remember back to Step 2: Observe, where you intentionally listened for the client's beliefs, language patterns, and metaphors. For example, *"My marriage is a nightmare"* or *"I never know when the next shoe is going to drop"* or *"I feel like I'm constantly walking on eggshells."* Nightmare, shoe drop, and eggshells are metaphors that carry a lot of rules, beliefs, and emotions within them. Someone walking on eggshells tells you they are anxious, nervous, fearful of upsetting someone, etc. This whole construct can be located as an energy/information pattern in or around the body. When you transform a metaphor—the way a client represents their world—you've hit the mother lode for transformation. Imagine the difference between "walking on eggshells" and "a walk in the park." In this example, we simply ask: *"Where, if anywhere, inside or outside the body is the information called walking on eggshells?"*

If the client has trouble expressing where the information is showing up, guide them to take another breath in, then try looking outside the body. Ask the question again: *"Where, if anywhere, outside the body, is information called _____ (emotion)?"*

Continue this process to identify where each emotional pattern presents.

Identify the Priority Pattern

Once the patterns are located and areas of the body have been identified, the next question is to determine which area of the body we are drawn to first. Once again, the body/subconscious will guide the order of priority, telling us which emotion wants our attention first.

Ask: *"Which area does the body want us to focus on first?"*

Honor the intelligence of the subconscious and how and what it chooses to communicate. It's critical to trust the body and the energy signals it's providing. If necessary, remind the conscious mind to step back and take notes. Remind the client to trust whatever shows up regardless of how strange or silly it might seem.

If there's difficulty identifying where to begin, choose one area and start there. If the subconscious does not agree, you will be immediately redirected. When the starting point has been set, we begin direct dialogue with this pattern as if it were an individual energy.

POINTer

The subconscious is highly literal. In a dialogue with the subconscious, trust what is being communicated, even if it doesn't make logical sense.

Inquiring with the Pattern

Now that you have mapped the patterns and know where to begin, it's time to inquire directly with the pattern. These questions follow a specific structure and sequence to reveal the pattern's original intention and explore the upsides and downsides.

As you engage in a dialogue with the subconscious, treat it with openness, objectivity, and respect. Talk to it the way you would talk to a favored friend or respected elder. Always use the exact wording the client uses. Do not interchange words just because there are other words you might use to explain a similar situation. Every word matters, and it never hurts to ask for permission!

Anxiety example: *"Anxiety, is that the name you go by or are you something different?"* (Wait for confirmation.) *"Is it ok if I ask you a few questions?"* (Wait for consent.)

In this dynamic, the client can "step outside of themselves," becoming a witness to what's being communicated to and through them.

Ask: *"Anxiety…how long have you been here? When did you first come to serve _____ (client name)?"*

Most people think their emotional reaction to current circumstances is new or unique to the situation at hand. In actuality, they are filtering current events through a protection pattern put in place a long, long time ago. Responses may include: *"since a particular age, since birth, forever, always, or possibly, for generations and lifetimes."*

Finding the Pattern's Intention

Next, we explore the pattern's purpose and intention.

Ask: *"_____ (pattern), what is your job? What are you here to do? What purpose do you serve?"*

Take notes on each response. The insights from this step will equip you to guide the release of a pattern that's no longer necessary, reengineer an existing pattern that chooses to upgrade, or install a completely new pattern.

Pay special attention to what I'm sharing with you here. The most common responses are: *"I'm here to protect, keep them safe, make sure they survive, make sure they don't fail, make sure they succeed, help them grow, help them fit in, make sure they are liked/loved, help them be strong, etc."* I hope you're getting the picture; these emotion patterns are here to protect and guide. Now that the client is hearing, in their own words, the intention behind these feelings, they begin to trust the feelings and realize they are advocates, not enemies. This sets the stage for us to go deeper.

POINTer

All emotion patterns have an upside; otherwise, they wouldn't stick.

Exploring the Upside and Downside

Getting to the heart of the intention behind any information pattern opens the door to discover the upside. Emotion patterns are set in the nervous system to serve a distinct purpose, including both a downside and an upside to their service. In the dialogue with the subconscious, the emotions *literally* express how they are causing suffering or distress (downside), as well as how they are trying to help and what information they want to share as a benefit (upside).

Ask: *"What are the gifts or character qualities that have been developed as a result of this pattern?"*

We are looking for positive learnings and strengths acquired and cultivated because of this pattern—attributes like determination, perseverance, drive, resourcefulness, compassion, and strength, to name a few. Now that we have connected these assets with this seemingly negative pattern, the client's perspective shifts. Instead of seeing this pattern as a limitation, it takes on the persona of an ally.

The next questions are: *"What is the upside or positive impact of these gifts? What are some of the results and benefits these gifts have produced?"*

In the anxiety example, the upside might sound like, *"She is always prepared, I help her stay organized, she works really hard to reach her goals, and we've gotten very good results; she just got promoted!"* Continue to ask questions of the same emotion until the upside has been fully expressed. (Note: the responses come back as the emotion speaking in the first person, the practitioner is the second person, and the client is the third person.)

Upside examples will vary dramatically from *"serving"* to *"able to handle any challenge"* to *"thriving"* to *"overcoming tremendous odds"* to *"focused and disciplined to achieve career or health and fitness success"* to *"fulfillment and happiness"* and everything in between.

So, what's the downside?

We've uncovered the upside and the client is beginning to see and experience the truth behind their feelings. We now want to uncover the downside of the pattern, this time from the subconscious mind's perspective. This is critical because without exposing the downside the subconscious is not motivated to change things.

Ask: *"What, if anything, has been the downside, something you didn't expect and certainly never intended?"*

In the anxiety example, the downside might sound like, *"I work her into a frenzy and stress her out"* or *"She gets so nervous she can't sleep, loses her appetite, and gets short-tempered with others."* We want to gather as much downside as we can so the desire to transform becomes a must.

Here are a few more examples of downsides: loss of confidence, hesitation, fear, feeling unworthy or unimportant, indecision, holding back, playing small, sacrificing oneself to gain acceptance, not taking action due to fear of failing, feeling the need to constantly improve oneself, the need to please everyone, and so on.

Reestablish the Pattern's Intention

The next questions are more rapid fire:

Ask: *"Was this your intention?"*

The answer is "No" about 97% of the time. In the anxiety example, the answer was *"No! I was trying to push her to succeed and help her achieve her outcomes; I didn't even think about those things."* (Note: If you choose to learn this method, you'll find out what to do when you don't get the answer you're hoping for.)

"What do you really want for _____ (client's name)?"

You'll get lots of beautiful answers to this question, and they usually relate to success, happiness, and well-being.

Inquire Recap

So far, you've relaxed the client and shifted them from the beta to theta brainwave state. Then you've identified which emotional patterns are presenting, where they're showing up in or around the body, and how long they've been serving the client. You learned the questions to ask to gain a true understanding of the pattern's intentions, the gifts it's given, as well as the upside and downside of its service. You also reestablished the pattern's ultimate intention. This new information from the subconscious becomes truth the conscious mind can logically understand and accept. The client is now able to see that anxiety had a positive intention and only wanted to serve them; it is no longer perceived as the enemy. There is now a recognition of the adverse consequences and an agreement that they are no longer acceptable, and it is high time for a change. Now you're ready to negotiate with the pattern which you will do in the next step of the P.O.I.N.T. method.

Inquire: Success Tips

- ◆ Ensure the client is sitting upright with their feet grounded on the floor and eyes closed.

- Maintain a gentle, low-volume tone of voice, using a slow, rhythmic pace.

- Allow yourself to relax into a slight trance as you begin the questioning process.

- Remind the client to respond aloud to all your questions.

- Follow the script until it becomes familiar enough to use from memory.

- When a client is having difficulty answering your questions, repeat all or parts of the script.

FreedomPOINT

STEP 4: NEGOTIATE

Now that the client has received the information from their subconscious mind and universal intelligence, the next step is to effectively communicate and negotiate with this information. The transition from Inquire to Negotiate happens once the pattern is open to changing. But how do we know *when* the subconscious is ready and willing? It's really quite brilliant. It's when there's a realization that the downside to running the pattern far outweighs the upside. Now the subconscious can *willingly* create a new strategy because the adverse consequences were never part of the original intent. Remember, the mind (conscious, subconscious, and unconscious), just like every other system in the body, is designed for and in service to your ultimate well-being.

POINTer

All emotions are in service to our basic human needs on some level, even when it doesn't feel like it. Just as every system in the body is working to support and sustain us in life, so is our emotional system.

At the end of Step 3, we asked if the pattern intended or wanted the downside, and the response was "No." Then we asked what the pattern really wanted for the client. This is the point at which the subconscious is willing and able to release the old pattern, upgrade the pattern to eliminate any "glitches," transform into another pattern, or install a brand-new pattern—here's where we negotiate.

This is the step where the bulk of the emotional transformation happens—where neurological patterns in the brain are re-engineered. This is happening within the subconscious, so just like the iceberg, or the butterfly's chrysalis, you may not physically see the transformation because it is hidden. The ultimate objective is to determine how to retain or expand the upside of the emotional patterns while resolving the downside.

In this step, we begin the negotiation by asking: *"If you could preserve the upside, would you?"* (99% of the time, the answer is a resounding "Yes!")

Now we are poised to guide the client through Step 4 and create a new, more empowering information pattern to take the place of the old, limiting pattern. We will design something completely aligned with the highest good of the individual with no carryover of the original downside.

POINTer

The subconscious mind continues to run the same programs/patterns on autopilot until it becomes aware of the downside and finds compelling reasons to change.

The negotiation occurs by finding out what each pattern needs to do to preserve the intended benefit and remove any downside. We refer back to the question from Step 3 where we reestablished the pattern's intention: *"What do you really want for _____ (client's name)?"*

Anxiety's response might sound something like, *"I want her to achieve. I want her to be successful. I want her to know she can do anything she sets her mind to! I want her to know that I am always here to help her find a way to thrive."*

Now ask the Negotiate questions:

1. *"Have you fulfilled your original intention?"*
   (If the answer is "Yes," ask):

2. *"Is it Ok for you to go now?"*
   (If the answer is "No," ask):

3. *"What do you need to change or add in order to fulfill the original intention and eliminate the downside?"*
   (e.g.: add confidence and self-trust and let go of the need for perfection)

POINTer

Negotiation is complete when the pattern has fulfilled its original intention, or the upside of the pattern is preserved.

The pattern has spoken out loud. Both the conscious mind and subconscious mind are fully aware of the desired outcome. They are also aware of the glitches (downside) in the original pattern/program. Internal conflicts are resolved, and all energy and information are aligned and ready to collaborate. It's time for transformation.

FreedomPOINT

STEP 5: TRANSFORM

In this step, patterns may be released (deleted), upgraded, or even combined with another to become a more supportive or powerful resource. To quicken and deepen the reorganization of neural pathways, we intensify the client's physical and emotional experience through intention and imagination. In doing so, we are technically amplifying the new energy frequency so that the vibration is felt in the body.

POINTer

Transformation can only happen if the original intention of the pattern is satisfied, or the upside of the pattern is preserved.

Proposing Options

Before proposing any options, be aware the subconscious will NOT release or transform any pattern until and unless the original intention is preserved or has been completely satisfied. Once this is confirmed, we can set up the options.

Option #1: Delete

We ask of the information pattern: *"Have you fulfilled your purpose? Is your mission complete?"* If the answer is "Yes," we ask: *"Is it ok for you to go now?"* The pattern may decide its work is done; it has accomplished what it set out to do and is now free to leave. If that's the case, we guide the release by saying, *"Now take a deep breath in, and with permission and intention, exhale and let it go."* (This may require 1-3 releasing breaths.)

Option #2: Install an Upgrade

The pattern may decide it wants to stay and serve the client a little longer, to change its strategy, or upgrade to a new level of service to the client. We ask: *"Is it time for you to go?"*

If the pattern says, "No! This person still needs me!" you can ask, *"Let's talk about how you'd like to serve them moving forward.* In the anxiety example, you might respond to the pattern: *"You said that some of the benefits are that she has become determined, dedicated, committed… If you've helped develop those gifts, would you want to continue serving her in that way?"*

Explore how the gifts resulting from this pattern may have been preparing to take the lead. We can ask the pattern if it has been mentoring these gifts, getting them ready for this very moment. We ask: *"Is it possible this is the next level of service you're able to offer? Are you ready to put all of your energy into amplifying this gift/strength you helped build?"*

The key here is to understand what the pattern can do to preserve the desired upside of its original intention and eliminate the downside. To set the stage for the subconscious to look for upside only, ask: *"What resource does _____ (client's name) need to go to the next level in their life?"* (They may need more self-confidence, courage, faith, or trust.)

"Would you like to redirect all of your energy into this resource?" If the answer is "Yes," we guide the upgrade by using intention and breathing.

"With intention, take a nice, deep breath, and as you exhale, complete the process."

Option #3: Install a New Program

It is common for patterns to want to blend with another existing emotion pattern or call in a new resource to enhance its ability to strengthen the upside and eradicate the downside. In some instances, the pattern will identify a resource it cannot find within the client. We ask: *"Is there a resource beyond what's currently available that needs to be called into service?"* This strategy is super fun because we invite the pattern and the client to locate the new resource in the quantum field/ infinite space, and with the next inhale, draw it into the body.

Expansion Option

For Option #2 and #3, once a pattern is upgraded or a new pattern is established, (for example, transforming anxiety into confidence), you want to increase the strength and presence of this new information. This is done by engaging the imagination and setting the intention to expand the new information throughout the body.

POINTer

While working with the subconscious, we engage imagination through intention and use breath to link the process to a physical action. Everything imagined in this work is as real to the subconscious as the nose on your face.

We instruct: *"Take a deep breath in, and as you exhale (with intention and permission alone), expand this information throughout every cell of the body. Now, allow it to become as big and powerful as it wants to be. Confidence, do you need to be even bigger or stronger to help _____* *(client's name) reach their potential and fulfill their dreams?"* If the answer is "Yes," we say, *"With the next breath, expand, multiply, magnify this new information 10X, 100X, 1000X, or more."*

Once the new pattern has become as powerful and expansive as it wants to be, we inquire: *"Describe what you're experiencing. What physical sensations are you noticing? What emotions are now present? How is this different from what you felt before the session?"*

Now that the new pattern is fully present, we ask: *"When you think about what was stressing or upsetting you (person/circumstance/event), how do you feel now?"*

Listen carefully to their response. What you're looking for here is diminished intensity, neutrality, or a completely different, more empowering feeling. You never want to make assumptions or personal judgments. It is possible that even after all the questioning and strategizing that occurred in the previous step, the pattern may still have some information left to share.

Testing the Transformation

The testing in this step is to check for any lingering information that may still be present to ensure the patterns are complete with their communication before the session concludes. In this final step, we revisit all the information patterns we charted on the body diagram. We address each location to check a few things:

♦ Is the original information (e.g.: anxiety) still present? If yes, to what degree of intensity?

Ask: *"On a scale of one to ten, how would you rate the current level of intensity?"*

Probe the old pattern as to what else it wants the client to know. What other valuable insight does it have that has yet to rise to the surface? Responses may sound like: *"She just needs to trust herself more"* or *"He needs to remember how powerful he is and that I am here to help give more strength whenever he wants to call on me."*

Ask: *"Anxiety, what additional information needs to be shared before you can go?"* (Repeat the message aloud back to the client.)

Ask: *"Has the message been received and accepted?"* If the answer is "Yes," ask: *"Is it ok for you to transform now?"*

♦ If the original information is no longer present:

Ask: *"What, if anything, has taken its place?"*

Ask: *"What message or advice does it wish to convey?* (Capture the message in your notes and reiterate to the client.)

Future Pace

Direct the client to step into the future one week from now. Then ask them to describe what, if anything, looks or feels different than it did before. How have their expanded emotional resources helped them experience more ease or happiness? Once you've reflected their response back to them, ask them to step into the future 30 days from now. Knowing they have been utilizing their new emotional patterns for a whole month, ask them to stop, reflect, and describe what has taken place in their life over the past 30 days.

Ask: *"What things have changed for you? In what ways have you personally benefited from your new patterns? What improvements have you noticed in your career? With your health? In your relationships? What's happening with the people around you?"*

A new truth will begin to unfold—the truth of the client's Ideal ME. Continue to compound the positive effects of their new patterns by stretching the imagination to step forward 90 days and paint a new picture. Then, expand the timeframe to a full year or even five years! How has the picture evolved and transformed?

POINTer

From just a few minutes of future pacing, the client will begin to create new possibilities for their Ideal ME they never dreamed were achievable.

Validating the Client's Transformation

Once the inception of the Ideal ME is fully underway, slowly and carefully bring the client back to consciousness in the present moment. Before they open their eyes, ask them to take a brief moment to notice the physical sensations in their body to help connect them with their own experience of transformation. They can validate how differently they feel now compared to how they felt at the beginning of the session.

POINTers to help guide the client in expressing their transformation:

"What are you feeling now?" (Lighter, radiant, relaxed, centered, calm, no tension)

"What emotions are now present?"

"What information do these emotions have for you to carry you into the future?"

(The subconscious might reply with affirmations like, *"We believe in you! You've got this! You're ready now!"*)

"How do you feel differently from when we began this conversation?"

"When you think about the old obstacles/situations, how do you feel about them now?"

"What insights or advice comes to you from this new information?"

As the session concludes, invite the client to take a deep breath in, exhaling slowly, and gently opening their eyes as they bring their attention back to the moment.

As a final question, we ask: *"Do you have any questions or comments?"*

The Litmus Test of Transformation

How do you know when transformation occurs? When the client no longer wants to do what they used to do, behave how they used to behave, or feel the distress they used to feel. Their priorities, rules, and values have shifted. Their desires have changed and something within them has been made new.

Let's recap:

Step 1: Prepare – Get yourself and your client ready for the session.

Step 2: Observe – Pay attention to the patterns creating stress, distress, or holding the client back. Look and listen for words through self-talk, language patterns, beliefs, metaphors, etc.

Step 3: Inquire – Ask specific questions designed to open the subconscious, facilitate the experience, and gather information about each pattern.

Step 4: Negotiate – Explore the upside and downside of each pattern. Strategize with the subconscious to preserve the upside and eliminate the downside.

Step 5: Transform – You've reached the POINT at which the subconscious is free to organize a new pattern by releasing it, upgrading it, combining with a new resource, or installing a brand-new pattern.

You now have the transformation system it took me nearly 20 years to perfect. I hope you'll use it to enrich your life and help uplift the people you are here to serve!

PART III

Client Transformation Stories

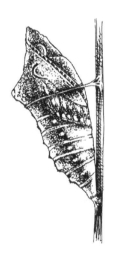

PART III

Client Transformation Stories

*"Just when the caterpillar thought the world was over,
it became a butterfly."*

—*Chuang Tzu*

A s YOU READ the following client stories, I invite you to consider the emotion patterns presented. Use the prompting questions on the journal pages at the end of each story to capture your thoughts about emotion patterns which might be affecting your ability to live with more ease and fulfillment.

Amy

Becoming a Feminine Superhero

Married with two children and living in Portland, Amy began experiencing disturbing emotional triggers of sadness, anger, and rage. She was also noticing a growing level of exaggerated fear and paranoia, particularly of men and the police, which activated a stutter in her speech.

POINTer

The first step in the P.O.I.N.T. method is to prepare yourself and the client for a successful session. Remember to practice the acronym FACE (Focus, Affirm, Center, Engage) to bring yourself into a state of presence and stillness. When your mind is fully present and focused in the now, there is a gap that is created in the mental thought process, causing the chatter of the mind to dissipate.

In using a gentle tone of voice while speaking slowly, Amy's anxious energy was calmed, and she was able to "land" in the space for her session. Supporting Amy with a calm environment allowed her to fully accept and embrace her emotions instead of resisting them.

POINTer

Resistance can add more layers of emotions, masking the core emotion(s) that are at the heart of the issue.

In the second step of Observation, as Amy and I conversed with the emotions and her pain points, I used active listening and asking questions to observe the patterns that were causing her distress. As she addressed each emotion, I only listened for the information associated with each obstacle, avoiding getting caught up in the details of the circumstances or stories. The primary question I always ask is, "How does that make you feel?"

Amy expressed several emotion patterns. Knowing that patterns do not always work in isolation, we slowly peeled back the layers of the onion to observe the various patterns which were linked with the core emotion(s). We moved past "bucket emotions" of anger, fear, and paranoia to identify feelings of rejection, inadequacy, and guilt. Amy expressed that as a child, she grew up with a father who was a Vietnam veteran who had physically abused her mother and sister. Having witnessed this familial abuse as a young girl, Amy felt terrified. Her mother felt unable to speak up and defend herself, and as a result, Amy unconsciously modeled her mother, developing a distrust in men over time. This distrust caused Amy to struggle to connect with her feminine energy. Even in her marriage, she had difficulty finding a comfortable balance with her masculine and feminine energy. Amy became a bodybuilder to increase her strength and ability to protect herself. One of the language patterns she used was "wanting to be able to go toe to toe with any man."

Amy shared she felt especially triggered by men who worked in positions of authority which generated an overall lack of trust and safety. When in situations where Amy felt a lack of control, her fear and anger became activated. She believed "she had rage in her own DNA that had been passed down for many generations." Amy described her anger outbursts feeling strangely familiar, like a déjà vu moment she was remembering from a past life. Amy would find herself becoming easily angered, yelling at her children, almost as if she was unable to control it, followed by feeling guilt and remorse afterwards.

In one session, she disclosed that she was creating irrational stories in her mind about the police coming to get her and her family and feared she wouldn't be able to do anything to protect herself or them. With the mounting societal racial tension, riots, and violence that was happening during this period of her life, the news and social media only seemed to exacerbate Amy's fear triggers. Her overactive emotional centers in the brain created exaggerated fear and paranoia.

Amy felt unsafe around men largely because of what she had witnessed in her family upbringing. She perceived females as weak, rejecting her own powerful feminine energy and focusing on becoming more masculine. In the movie of her life, she believed that men have the control, so instead of being a strong female lead character who can tap into her feminine power, she adopted a more masculine persona to protect herself.

The downside of suppressing her feminine energy and fearing the masculine was that Amy became unable to express love and trust in her intimate relationships. She couldn't fully surrender to a partner and feel safe with them. Another downside (paranoia) was her tendency to focus on what she was afraid of, ultimately spiraling into imagining the worst possible scenarios. Paranoia represents a heightened sense of awareness with the brain attempting to differentiate what's real and what's not. The upside to paranoia forces you to pay close attention to what's real and what's not so you can discover a new reality. Amy felt she was powerless with a man unless she met his masculinity with her own. The upside was that she faced her fear head on, and through embodying masculine energy, she developed her physical strength and confidence, allowing her to powerfully interact with men; it was an effort to reclaim her power. Paranoia forced her to question, "Is this fearful belief really true?" Questioning whether the reality she was living was true was really a benefit for Amy. She realized she didn't find more safety or trust in becoming more masculine; in fact, it was the opposite. Her subconscious was urging her to find that same power through her feminine energy. Being a strong woman was her superpower.

We all have both masculine and feminine energy, and when they are in balance, we thrive.

POINTer

The subconscious mind (operating system) will continue to run the same pattern until the pattern is deleted, upgraded, or a new one is installed.

Amy is now able to find inner peace by feeling safe and being able to trust. Rather than being fearful of men, Amy began to perceive all human beings as connected souls who are here to help one another grow and evolve and to teach, not to harm. Where Amy used to fear, judge, and retreat from her emotion patterns, she is now more open to exploring the information they want to share in serving her highest good. Amy describes the body-scanning process in P.O.I.N.T. like a map which directs her straight to the core distressing emotion so she can communicate with it safely and objectively with the intention to understand its strategy, enabling her to release or transform it to be of better service to her.

Journal

- Where, if anywhere, in your life have you experienced a fear of trusting or expressing love in an intimate relationship?
- "Bucket emotions" often mask other core emotions that lie beneath the surface. Take a bucket emotion such as stress, anger, or fear and explore what other emotion patterns might be contributing to the bucket emotion.

Angie B.

Getting Back into the Game

Angie B. had been a very confident, driven, successful sales professional who had a high income-producing management role within her company. In her late 50s, her position was suddenly eliminated, so she made the decision to make a fresh start by taking her career in a new direction. Angie B. joined her husband in a new business venture, and they moved to a new state. Her professional achievements had contributed significantly to her identity, and like many of us, she depended on her career and her marriage for certainty and security. After a second move and several years of being away from her sales career, Angie B. and her husband divorced, and she decided to get back into the industry she had left. During this tumultuous transition period, she developed some very common emotion patterns that often occur when life deals a difficult hand: loss of confidence, anxiety and uncertainty about the future, and fear of survival.

Not only had she been "out of the sales game" for several years, but she was also living in a new place where her reputation for being successful was largely unknown. Not that long ago, she was at the top of her career and had established a dedicated professional network that would be ready and willing to hire her for a position at the management level she was qualified for. Instead, as Angie B. began looking for opportunities in a new market, her previous identity was challenged. Rather than being embraced and praised for her achievements, she was met with skepticism and doubt: "Why did you decide to leave this industry? What makes you want to reengage now? A lot has changed in the past several years...you'll have some catching up to do to prove yourself." Angie B.'s belief in herself began to wane significantly. Had she lost her mojo? Would she really have to prove herself like a rookie when she had already accomplished so much in her career?

Remember, our beliefs have written the story of "who we think we are," so when our grounding in those beliefs is shaken by unforeseen circumstances, the subconscious mind can devise some very complex emotional strategies to help us remember who we are. On a conscious level, trying to logically "figure out" the next step can be quite daunting and scary. Although the circumstances are different, you can see how Angie B.'s story can easily relate to professionals who choose to leave their careers to have children and stay at home for a period, returning to judgment and scrutiny when ready to reenter the workplace. This is why the story or circumstances can be helpful in understanding the background of emotion patterns, but *how the circumstances make you feel is the primary focus*. It's not the divorce or career causing the distress; it's the feeling of fear, self-doubt, uncertainty, and lack of confidence that need to be spoken with.

POINTer

Fear often shows up when there is a lack of focus or feeling scattered, so getting centered and feeling prepared are key factors in minimizing fear-based patterns.

We are faced with so many challenges and changes in life which can bring about massive levels of uncertainty that shake us to our core. What's important to know is that the upside of the emotion of fear is about getting centered and focused when you feel scattered or unprepared.

Being prepared and getting reacquainted with how her industry had evolved in the years she had been away was an important step for Angie B. to feel confident and ready for her upcoming interview. To overcome her self-doubt, she needed to tap back into her strengths and youthful energy, as well as reconnect with the self-confidence she had forgotten.

POINTer

In the Inquire step of the process, having the conversation with the emotion pattern(s) is essentially what releases the resistance and tension.

We've been conditioned as to which emotions are acceptable to express and which ones are not, so as a result, we often suppress, repress, avoid, or numb the ones that feel negative or distressing. In doing this, we do ourselves a world of disservice because in avoiding the pattern(s), we become blind to the true intention and upside. In the Inquire step, tension can be released because the emotions have finally been communicated with and given permission to be explored, accepted, and understood. The effort in holding them captive is dropped; they are free to exist and be felt.

Inquire Conversation:

> Deb: *"Where, if anywhere, inside or outside the body, is information called Unconfident?"*
>
> Angie B.: *"In my lower back and sciatica."*
>
> Deb: *"Unconfident, is it ok if I ask you a few questions?"*
>
> Unconfident: *"Yes."*
>
> Deb: *"Unconfident, how long have you been here? When did you first come to serve Angi B.?"*
>
> Unconfident: *"Since she was 5 years old."*

Deb: *"Unconfident, what job did you come to do?"*

Unconfident: *"To help her shine by building back her confidence and certainty and prompt her to go prepare and practice. Also, to help her do her best and prove that she can get back in the game and succeed."*

Deb: *"Unconfident, what has been the benefit of your service?" How have you come to help Angie B.?"*

Unconfident: *"I help her to be focused, prepared, and centered."*

Deb: *"Unconfident, what, if anything, is the downside of your service?"*

Unconfident: *"I cause her self-doubt, worry, anxiety, fear, and uncertainty."*

Deb: *"Unconfident, are there any more downsides of your service?"*

Unconfident: *"She questions her capability and feels afraid. When she's fearful instead of being focused and prepared, she hesitates or just focuses on what could go wrong."*

Deb: *"So, Unconfident, anxiety, self-doubt, and feeling afraid… is that what you ultimately intended for her?"*

Unconfident: *"No."*

Negotiate Conversation:

Deb: *"Unconfident, have you fulfilled your original intention?"*

Unconfident: *"No."*

Deb: *"What do you need to change or add in order to fulfill the original intention and eliminate the downside?"*

Unconfident: *"Stronger confidence, more faith, and to reconnect with all sources of her power."*

For Angie B., the intention of the information called Unconfident was there to prompt her to take the steps she needed to remember that her certainty and confidence are always available within. Fear was simply helping her get prepared. She had been out of the game for a while, so she did need to study, prepare, and get reacquainted with her industry.

Angie B. reconnected with all her sources of strength and power, which were integrated into one force, one identity. In doing so, she was able to reconnect with her past success and magnify her self-confidence when she needed it. When she interviewed with a panel of five senior management-level people, she went into the interview feeling light, playful, self-assured, prepared, and very focused. She recalled feeling an inner peace throughout the entire interview process.

Angie B. got the job she wanted and earned multiple six figures in her first year back in her sales industry. Now, she can easily ground herself in her power identity if she begins to feel worry, doubt, or fear in any area of her life.

Journal

- As a child, which emotions were you taught or conditioned to suppress, repress, avoid, or numb?
- What external areas in your life have you depended upon for certainty and security? (e.g.: job, relationship, family, etc.)
- In what ways and under what circumstances has your self-confidence been tested? What can you identify as the upside of the pattern?

....
....
....
....
....
....
....
....
....
....
....
....
....
....
....
....
....
....
....

Lu

Enough is Enough

I met Lu when she was in her late 50s. She was a very beautiful, highly qualified, and well-respected physician, but the emotion pattern of not being good enough was holding her back from finding personal fulfillment and reaching her greatest potential in several areas of her life.

Lu's need to please other people had been something she'd lived with from a very early age. As a young child, Lu had formed the belief that if someone pays attention to you and takes good care of you, that means they love you, and the reverse was just as true. This belief played out in Lu's movie called *Will I Ever Be Enough?* and she cast herself in the lead role of Peacemaker and People Pleaser.

Being the peacemaker of her family and making sure everyone was happy was a subconscious strategy to provide Lu with the assurance that she was loved. The reality she had created from her subconscious programming generated experiences that caused her to struggle with a lack of self-love and self-belief. Needing to please others was causing Lu to feel inauthentic and unable to speak up for her own needs and desires. The more she isolated herself in fear of rejection, the more desperate for connection she became. Lu had developed so much self-doubt about her ability to be good enough, she lost her ability to be open and vulnerable because it simply didn't feel safe. The absence of love felt safer than opening her heart to someone new. Not being able to please them and eventually suffering rejection for not being good enough could leave her with a broken heart and feeling unloved.

Lu often experienced feeling not good enough in her profession, and the emotional distress was even greater when it came to her romantic relationships. For years, as a single mother and high-performing physician, Lu was finding less and less time for dating and social gatherings. With each day that passed, her fear of not being loved and never being able to find a lasting loving romantic relationship mounted. The walls of emotional protection grew taller and thicker. She wondered; will I ever find someone? Do I deserve love and happiness? Have I done enough? Am I pretty enough? Can I really have it all? Am I worthy of the love I desire?

In our session, we also had a conversation with the emotion pattern of judgment. Lu judged herself as being unworthy. It's the feeling of unworthiness that causes a pattern of never feeling like enough, no matter how kind, generous, beautiful, or successful one is. Not only was Lu judging herself and whether she would ever be good enough to be in a loving relationship, she was also transferring that judgment onto other people.

Inquire Conversation:

> Deb: *"Where, if anywhere, inside or outside the body, is information called Unworthiness?"*
>
> Lu: *"In my heart."*
>
> Deb: *"Unworthiness, is it ok if I ask you a few questions?"*
>
> Unworthiness: *"Yes."*
>
> Deb: *"Unworthiness, how long have you been here? When did you first come to serve Lu?"*

Unworthiness: *"Since she was 3 years old."*

Deb: *"Unworthiness, what job did you come to do?"*

Unworthiness: *"My purpose is to help her achieve and succeed at a high level to show her she's so capable and so worthy. She can do anything."*

Deb: *"Unworthiness, what has been the benefit of your service?" How have you come to help Lu?"*

Unworthiness: *"I help Lu be committed, focused, organized, and successful. I give her lots of stamina to make that level of success possible."*

Deb: *"And what else are you here to do for her?"*

Unworthiness: *"I want to show her how worthy she is of her own love and receiving the love and admiration of others."*

Deb: *"Unworthiness, what, if anything, is the downside of your service?"*

Unworthiness: *"She's so focused on trying to prove she's enough and striving to achieve that she doesn't focus on the love surrounding her or nurturing herself and her relationships. She's exhausted and lonely."*

Deb: *"Unworthiness, are there any more downsides of your service?"*

Unworthiness: *"She's not able to enjoy the present moment and is always looking into the future for happiness. She has a fear of commitment and intimate relationships, and she's resistant to men in general."*

Deb: *"So, Unworthiness, Lu never feeling enough, judging herself and others, cutting off relationships and opportunities, missing out on loving relationships and committing to a man...*

is that what you ultimately intended for her?”

Unworthiness: *“No.”*

Deb: *“Unworthiness, what do you really want for Lu? If you could give her anything in the whole world, what would it be? What would you want to do for her?”*

Unworthiness: *“I would give Lu courage to be vulnerable, authentic, and open so she could attract the man of her dreams and have a lasting and loving relationship. I want her to recognize how incredible she is and to feel so proud of all she’s achieved in her life. I want her to feel like she can be her authentic self all the time and know that she’s always been enough.”*

In the process of identifying both the upside and downside, Lu accepted the benefits (upside) of the pattern, as well as her brand-new awareness of how it’s causing unnecessary suffering (downside). The next step is to negotiate with the pattern.

POINTer

In the Negotiate step, internal conflicts are resolved by finding out what each pattern needs to do to preserve the intended benefit and remove any downside.

Negotiate Conversation:

Deb: *“Have you fulfilled your original intention?”*

Unworthiness: *“Yes”*

Deb: *“Unworthiness, is it time for you to go and give way to courage, vulnerability, and authenticity?”*

Unworthiness: *“Yes!”*

As unworthiness was released and set free and the new patterns of courage, vulnerability, and authenticity were amplified, Lu realized it was safe to love herself and accept her strengths and weaknesses without comparing herself to the rest of the world. Lu was guided to reconnect with her internal confidence and power that were inside of her all along. She made the decision to begin enjoying the present moment, not looking to the future for happiness or blocking herself from love.

Lu began online dating and hired a matchmaker. She wore a special outfit on her dates that made her feel beautiful and confident. After dating multiple men, she met a man who thought the world of her and treated her like a queen. Lu is no longer hesitant or afraid of being in a loving relationship. She has more self-confidence than ever before and describes feeling fearless to go for what she wants in life. To reconnect with her femininity, she has a ritual of putting on her favorite pair of red stiletto heels as she leaves the office and heads home to remind herself to embrace self-love and her inner and outer beauty.

Journal

- Internally or externally, where, if anywhere, have you experienced feelings of unworthiness? How can you relate to the upside and downside of Lu's story?
- Describe the possible upsides and downsides of being a peacemaker or people pleaser.

....

....

....

....

....

....

....

....

....

....

....

....

....

....

....

....

....

....

....

Jamie

Overcoming Overwhelm

I began working with Jamie while he was working in a family business he co-owned with his father. Although Jamie and his father built their business together, Jamie didn't receive the respect and authority he deserved from his father, which led to debilitating emotion patterns of perfectionism and a severe fear of failure. Jamie worked long hours each day, passionate to produce results, but he found himself second-guessing his decisions and lacking confidence in the way he communicated with his team. Jamie was never quite satisfied with his present success; he was always looking to the future and focusing on what more he needed to accomplish to feel successful and prove to his father that he was capable of running the business.

POINTer

In Step 2 of P.O.I.N.T. (Observe), as the conversation progresses, you are observing the emotion patterns. In identifying and naming the emotions, you become crystal clear on what specific patterns are at play, and typically there are more than one.

Jamie initially expressed he wanted to be able to make more confident business decisions and relieve the pressure of having to prove himself to his father. In the Observation segment of the conversation, Jamie shared that, as a child, he felt rejected and undermined by both of his parents and rarely received much praise from them, especially his father. Over the course of his life, Jamie began repressing his feelings of not being good enough, feeling more and more judged with every decision he made, which eventually led to a deeply rooted fear of failure, overwhelm, and a pattern of stress-filled overachieving at all costs. He described a very dark period in his life where the overwhelm and fear had pushed him to the point of "hitting rock bottom...feeling as if he was going to crack." He had even engaged in behaviors of self-harm and was losing his will to live. The downside of overwhelm, overachieving, fear of failure, not being good enough, and fear of rejection had become so intense, they were literally unbearable for Jamie to live with.

Over many years, Jamie and I had multiple sessions together, peeling back the onion of various compounding emotion patterns. In one session, we spoke directly with his pattern of overwhelm and perfectionism. Jamie's subconscious communicated that the upside of these emotions was to protect him and prepare him to be successful, to ensure he achieved his desired results in his business.

POINTer

Overwhelm is almost always closely linked with prioritization and organization.

Overwhelm practically forces you to assess everything that's on your to-do list, then prioritize what to tackle first and organize a plan to get it all done. The downside is that when overwhelm is repressed and ignored, it becomes debilitating, leading to procrastination, stagnation, and feeling defeated.

There's an interesting aspect of emotion pattern strategy in the subconscious: when the strategy isn't working—when it's not getting the intended outcome in its service to us—the subconscious doesn't automatically look for a new strategy; rather, the existing pattern simply works harder to fulfill the original strategy. This is the reason for asking the pattern about its original intention for the client: "What would you want Jamie to know where he could benefit from all of the upside and eliminate the downside?"

POINTer

The subconscious is ready and willing to transform the pattern when the downside(s) to running the pattern far outweigh the upside(s).

In the Transformation conversation of Step 5, when it was time to reconcile the pattern, Jamie's subconscious chose Option #2: Install an Upgrade. It created a new identity by combining the resources of Sound Judgment and Wise Beliefs that he could call on at any time to step into his power and draw the energy and confidence he needed. These resources took on the image of a "power generator" as the ultimate source of energy he needed to get his work completed with ease, eliminating the need for stress and overwhelm.

As with most clients, resolving an emotion pattern in one area of life transfers into other areas as well. In Jamie's case, he later reported that his new "business power generator" reference also enabled him to perform better and with more strength in his workouts at the gym. Jamie is now able to make decisions more quickly and confidently without second-guessing himself. In taking over the family business from his father, Jamie reports the business is performing better now than ever before. With his team, Jamie's old pattern of communicating in a very non-confrontational way has shifted into communicating with more clarity, confidence, and direction. He has implemented a habit of appreciating and celebrating the smaller business wins, which keeps his overachieving and perfectionism at bay. Jamie has expressed he has been able to go to the next level in multiple areas of his life by calling on his power generator. In releasing many of his stuck emotion patterns, Jamie has a new appreciation for life and sleeps longer and more restfully. He also noticed that the wrinkles he had between his eyebrows resulting from stress and worry have disappeared and jokingly refers to FreedomPOINT as "Botox without the chemicals."

Journal

🦋 In what areas of your life do you experience emotion patterns of overwhelm, overachieving, or fear of failure?

🦋 What emotion resources might you combine to create your own "power generator?"

....
....
....
....
....
....
....
....
....
....
....
....
....
....
....
....
....
....
....
....
....
....
....

G.S.

From Queen of Procrastination to Queen of Action

When G.S. came to me, she was happy with her marriage, family, and career, but felt that "something was still missing." G.S. and her husband own a martial arts studio where they teach self-defense classes, and she's passionate about educating on women's empowerment. G.S. expressed having difficulty stepping into her power as a leader and speaker—"playing small" regarding her life mission and purpose. Her personality and energy are so vibrant; she lights up every room she walks into, but when she thinks about presenting in front of a large group of people, her light immediately dims, and her confidence diminishes.

G.S. envisioned becoming a successful speaker and personal development coach, but she had developed some major reluctance to pursuing her dream because of her language fluency. English wasn't her primary language, which caused an immense lack of confidence, especially when asked to speak in front of large groups. Additionally, she was diagnosed with ADHD (Attention-deficit/hyperactivity disorder) as a child and lacked confidence in her learning abilities.

As the main supporter and caretaker of her family, she described herself as "always the muse and never the artist." She used the metaphor of "being at a crossroads" about making business decisions, fearing she wasn't doing enough to succeed. She also described feeling "stuck in her mind," focused on how others would judge her. Fear and procrastination were holding her back from moving toward being the leader she truly wanted to be, and she labeled herself "The Queen of Procrastination."

POINTer

Procrastination is very closely linked with perfectionism. Those who seek perfection have trouble taking action toward their goals, fearing the potential rejection or unacceptance from others.

Oftentimes, clients who feel stuck and struggle to move forward toward a particular outcome ask themselves the question "Is what I want really worth the effort?" This question only adds fuel to the fire, leading to more procrastination. What is hiding under the perceived laziness is in fact an avoidance of rejection and potentially even humiliation.

G.S.' emotion patterns were reluctance, focusing on the negative, and lack of confidence, which were expressed as playing small and procrastinating. The downside of G.S.' procrastination was that it was only delaying the real problem; it increased tension and stress, making her feel guilty for not taking action, which then developed into judging herself as unworthy. The higher intention (upside) of focusing on the negative was to show her what she doesn't want; it was only there to create contrast and to motivate her to change her mindset. Most people don't realize that contrast, or knowing what you *don't* want, is really there to help them recognize what they *do* want in their lives. Instead, people tend to get hung up by continuing to focus on the negative. Contrast is a gift because it shows what is truly wanted and strengthens us to go after it.

Reluctance of taking the lead and stepping into a leadership role came to strengthen G.S.' character. Wisdom has been with her all her life; she knew what others needed and how to support them, but she feared the responsibility. She needed to grow her strength to go from being the supporter to the leader. The intention of reluctance was to show her that regardless of the culture and conditioning she grew up in, the power to lead is and was always inside of her. Stepping up and moving past her own reluctance was the very act of female empowerment she was teaching others. The emotion pattern of procrastination urged G.S. to use her wisdom and creativity to figure out how to make the best use of her time, allowing her to accomplish more with less stress and more fluidity.

Her subconscious shared the upside of her ADHD. The intention was to make sure she didn't miss anything and to help her imagination take hold, giving her mind more freedom to create. Imagination helps create inner vision to keep her growing, expanding her abilities, and to direct her energy toward her purpose.

The emotion patterns of reluctance, procrastination, playing small, and lack of confidence expressed their desire to help G.S. break through her self-imposed limitations by expanding her strength of creativity, ability to easily adapt to her circumstances, and take expedient, intelligent action toward her goals. By the end of her session, G.S. moved from "The Queen of Procrastination" to the "Queen of Action." Her intelligence, wisdom, inner certainty, and faith were all magnified from a level three to a level ten.

Although one session is without a doubt transformational, multiple sessions are encouraged because, inevitably, more emotions will bubble up and transformations will continue. Often in the first session, the objective is to reveal the protection mechanisms and create more empowering strategies for the client. In G.S.' next session, we addressed the pattern of wasting time. Reluctance had come with an intention to show her she could accomplish more in less time and with less stress, yet G.S. acknowledged she was not being organized or efficient. The pattern of wasting time had been with her almost her whole life and it caused her to become easily distracted and stressed.

What G.S.' higher intelligence wanted her to understand is that we all have 24 hours in a day, but it is how you use that time that makes all the difference. The pattern said, "This is the time of your life! Life is a game with an unknown timer on it." Her subconscious helped her recognize and appreciate the power and value of time. "Wasting time" was then transformed into "smart use of time." That created a transfer of power which immediately generated more organization and efficiency.

"Smart use of time" chose to expand into "making smart choices overall," which extended into G.S.' health and fitness habits. She began making smarter choices, and by the following session, G.S. had dropped the extra weight she had gained. This was the time of her life, and she chose to improve her diet, get out in nature, and work out more regularly without making it an assignment or obligation.

Whether on stage or off, G.S. is now able to feel more confident, more playful, more present, more assertive, and more at ease in her leadership communication. She has expressed, "There's nothing I can't do now!"

Journal

❧ In what circumstances has procrastination and playing small shown up in your life experiences?

❧ How has perfectionistic behavior affected your ability to take action and move forward?

....
....
....
....
....
....
....
....
....
....
....
....
....
....
....
....
....
....
....
....
....
....

Irena

It's Me Against the World

Irena is a clinical psychologist who approached me at an event, explaining how, for years, she was having trouble finding joy and gratitude in her life and didn't know why or how to fix it. Irena had studied many religious practices, spiritual modalities, and invested in personal development coaching to help her reclaim the beauty of her life, but nothing provided her with lasting results.

In Step 2 (Observe), Irena shared that she was born in the Soviet Union and her mother became very sick after giving birth, causing Irena to be separated from her mother for nearly a month. The hospital nurses didn't take great care of her, and Irena developed a severe skin rash from not having her diapers changed often enough. As a young child, Irena would wake up every morning with a heavy heart, wondering, "What do I have in my life that I could lose today? How can I hold onto the little bit that I have?" She used the term "counting her chickens," feeling afraid of losing everyone and everything that mattered in her life. This fear was causing mounting levels of anxiety and feeling disconnected from her ability to thrive in the world. In fact, she had a mantra that stemmed from her difficult childhood of "It's me against the world." To Irena, the world was not a friendly place.

When Irena birthed her first child, she recalled that her happiness was almost immediately overtaken by her subconscious pattern of feeling worried about what might happen to her new baby. Irena's fear of losing her loved ones became a looming pattern causing severe pain and distress in her life. She began a practice of giving gratitude every morning and as many times a day as she could, but there remained a dark shadow reminding her that she could lose it all at any moment. Even in times when good fortune came her way and life seemed to be flowing smoothly, Irena's joy and gratitude was fleeting, and her feelings of emptiness and anticipation of loss would re-emerge.

POINTer

The subconscious mind is the emotional hub which houses our inner intelligence, seamlessly connecting us with the all-knowing intelligence of universal energy.

In Step 3 of P.O.I.N.T. (Inquire), the conscious mind is given permission to take a step back so that the subconscious mind can step forward. When the brain is operating in theta frequency, we can more acutely access the subconscious mind, very old or repressed memories, and a "higher intelligence." It's not our job to judge what information comes through, only to trust that the information coming through has the intention to benefit the client in some way. In scanning the body for truth, we discover how miraculously it communicates, be it through distinct sensory feelings of pain, tingles, hairs standing up on the back of the neck, involuntary muscle twitches, goosebumps, or just a sudden inner knowing or intuitive instinct.

In asking Irena where inside or outside the body the information called "emptiness" was, she was led to her solar plexus chakra (stomach area under the sternum), then described the information as "a cold, bottomless black hole that sucks all the joy out of my life."

Inquire Conversation:

Deb: *"Where, if anywhere, inside or outside the body, is information called Emptiness?"*

Irena: *"I feel a black hole in my solar plexus."*

Deb: *"Emptiness, is it ok if I ask you a few questions?"*

Emptiness: *"Yes."*

Deb: *"Emptiness, how long have you been here? When did you first come to serve Irena?"*

Emptiness: *"I came to her in the hospital, when she was less than a month old."*

Deb: *"And Emptiness, what job did you come to do? What is your highest purpose to serve her?"*

Emptiness: *"I am an ancient energy—a black hole that came to protect baby Irena."*

Deb: *"Ancient energy, may I refer to you as Emptiness?"*

Emptiness: *"Please call me Protector."*

Deb: *"Okay, beautiful, thank you. Protector, what has been the upside of your service?"* In what ways have you come to help Irena?"*

Protector: *"When she was alone in the hospital, I placed a black hole around her solar plexus to protect her life-force energy."*

Deb: *"And what else are you here to do for her?"*

Protector: *"Ensuring her survival."*

Deb: *"Protector, what, if anything, is the downside of your service?"*

Protector: *"She's scared of losing people. Her anticipation of loss makes her feel afraid to fall in love…and she's very unhappy."*

Negotiate Conversation:

Deb: *"Protector, have you fulfilled your original intention?"*

Protector: *"Yes."*

Deb: *"So, Protector, does Irena still need your services?"*

Protector: *"No, she is ready to move forward."*

Deb: *"Protector, it sounds like you're ready to be released, is that right?"*

Protector: *"Yes."*

Transformation Conversation:

Deb: *"Protector, we thank you for your service to Irena for all these years. You have permission to leave."*

Deb: *"Now Irena, take a deep breath in, and with permission and intention, exhale and let it go."*

POINTer

Transformation can only happen if the original intention of the pattern is satisfied or the upside of the pattern is preserved.

In Step 5 (Transform), the pattern chose Option #1: Delete. The solution provided by her subconscious was to fill the hole with pure love and light repeatedly until the hole had completely disappeared. After Irena's session, she expressed feeling immediately relieved and happy. After some time had passed, Irena reported in a follow-up call that she felt a

75% improvement after her first session. She shared that although she had experienced occasional periods of feeling emptiness, her session gave her the ability to meet those moments head on, without feeling fearful or overwhelmed. Irena had developed the tools to move right through them by getting into a relaxed state, locating where the pattern is showing up in her body, and moving it straight into her head where she can consciously recognize and accept its presence. Then she can acknowledge that it is only there to remind her to send herself more love and positive energy. Finally, she can release it and let it go. Irena is no longer afraid of death and loss. She has allowed joy and gratitude to be magnified in her life where, rather than feeling that it's her against the world, the world is now on her side.

Journal

- In what ways, if any, can you identify emotion patterns in your life that may have led to feelings of emptiness or lack of joy?
- How might these emotion patterns served to protect you?

Jolene

Itching to Please

Jolene was a massage therapist in her early 30s when she was referred to me for a session. She had been dealing with a host of physical symptoms, which included migraine headaches, TMJ, a hernia, and severe eczema flare-ups caused by anxiety and emotional stress. As a young child, Jolene's parents became very ill, and she was forced to take over as the family caretaker. She had witnessed domestic abuse, codependent behavior, and sexual abuse as a child, which led to her inability to set appropriate boundaries in most areas of her life. In her profession, with her family, and in social settings, Jolene's tendency was to put everyone else's needs before her own. Throughout her life, the movie she had been acting in was written around the premise that the world isn't safe, so she developed a pattern of people pleasing and adapting to others to feel accepted and protected.

POINTer

When we experience threatening situations as a child, our subconscious creates certain strategies to feel safe, secure, appreciated, and accepted.

There is a well-known phrase: "There's safety in numbers." The quicker you become a part of a group, the threat of being harmed within that group diminishes significantly. We overextend and exhaust our energy to please others because, deep down, we don't feel safe and certain. This pattern is also commonly identified in situations of martyrdom.

In theta state, Jolene's subconscious revealed that her people-pleasing pattern had been around for many lifetimes and passed down for generations through her maternal lineage. She had cast herself as a martyr in her life movie just like her mother, grandmother, and so on.

Without realizing it, by learning to please others, Jolene was creating a world around her that felt safe and secure. The upside of her physical symptoms was that Jolene became a sort of chameleon. Because of her practiced adaptability, she was readily welcomed into virtually any environment, pleasing whoever was in need. Aside from the obvious physical pain and discomfort, the downside of these patterns was that Jolene lacked the ability to establish clear boundaries in her relationships. If a client needed a massage on a day where Jolene's schedule was booked solid, she would do whatever it took to fit them in.

During the conversation with her subconscious regarding her patterns around feeling unsafe, Jolene found herself sitting at a boardroom table, along with all the physical ailments she had been experiencing. Each of her physical symptoms had their own seat at the table. She described them as "very civilized and insightful as to why they had come to serve her in their various ways." She laughed at how some of the symptoms took form: one was a fuzzy, semi-transparent entity that was just a color, and another appeared as a silly-looking whack-a-mole. She even felt that in some way, the physical symptoms represented her relatives or ancestors who she finally had the opportunity to meet and have a conversation with.

POINTer

As a FreedomPOINT facilitator, there is no room for judgment as to what the subconscious mind shares; it's all just information. Consider that the client's brain is in theta, which is a dream-like state, and dreams often make no sense to our logical conscious mind. Accept and allow whatever comes up through the session.

Jolene's subconscious created a boardroom setting, allowing her to discover the higher purpose of her physical ailments in a safe, controlled environment. She described the boardroom meeting as relaxed, gentle, loving, and very insightful. She learned that her eczema was a response to feeling that the world is unsafe, which resulted in over-extending and over-giving, as well as not setting or maintaining healthy boundaries. We released the pattern of information called Unsafe that identified itself in her hands.

In Step 5 of P.O.I.N.T. (Transform), the emotion may be released, or it will express that it is still showing up somewhere.

Transformation Conversation:

> Deb: *"On a scale of one to ten, with ten being the most intense, how would you rate the emotion's current level of intensity?"*
>
> Jolene: *"One."*

At this stage you can probe the pattern as to what else it wants the client to know. What other valuable insight might it have that has yet to rise to the surface?

> Deb: *"Unsafe, is there anything else you want Jolene to know?"*
>
> Unsafe: *"She is always taken care of, and everything is working out for her highest good. She is loved and guided, always. It's okay for her to say no and take time for herself. The most important person to please is herself!"*

Now that the old patterns have been released and new ones have been installed, Jolene's subconscious is free to create new experiences by engaging her imagination. There are no limitations. No fixed beliefs. The subconscious is given a blank canvas to paint the picture of how life could look in a brand-new way.

> Deb: *"Jolene, I want to invite you to step into the future one week from now and describe what you see and how you feel, now that Unsafe has been released."*
>
> Jolene: *"I have so much energy. I also feel calmer and more relaxed. My hands are healing and have stopped itching. I'm taking the time I need for myself, and I still am succeeding in my business."*
>
> Deb: *"That sounds wonderful! Let's take things a step further and look forward to 30 days from now. What things have changed for you? In what ways have you personally benefited from your new patterns? What improvements have you noticed in your career? With your health? In your relationships? What's happening with the people around you?"*
>
> Jolene: *"My life looks and feels so different. I feel an inner peace, knowing that I am safe in the world. I'm in charge of my schedule and I include time to relax and enjoy life on my own terms. I feel confident in establishing boundaries with my clients, friends, and family members. My eczema has totally healed! I have made more money this month while working less hours. My relationships are so much better because I have time to enjoy the special people in my life."*

Within the same day as her session, Jolene reported that her hands had stopped itching, and within 24 hours, her skin had already begun to heal. Within two weeks of her session, her eczema was completely gone and hasn't returned in over 13 years. Occasionally, she gets a faint itch on her hands, which, according to Jolene, is a gift that serves as a reminder that she's allowing her boundaries to slip in some area of her life where she's pushing herself too hard or ignoring when she's in need of some self-love and self-care.

Journal

🦋 Where, if anywhere, have you struggled to set appropriate boundaries in your life?

🦋 Emotion patterns such as martyrdom and putting others first are strategies to keep you feeling safe and secure. What boundaries can you set that will honor your own needs and self-care?

....

....

....

....

....

....

....

....

....

....

....

....

....

....

....

....

....

....

....

PART IV

Your P.O.I.N.T. Journey

PART IV

Your P.O.I.N.T. Journey

"When a caterpillar bursts from its cocoon and discovers it has wings, it does not sit idly, hoping to one day turn back. It flies."

—*Kelseyleigh Reber*

Begin Your FreedomPOINT Journey Now!

The P.O.I.N.T. method is extremely powerful work when guided by a certified practitioner, but you can still make massive progress in transforming your emotional patterns by journaling your experience, which will help you implement all you've learned in this book. Perhaps you're dealing with fear, insecurity, confusion, frustration, anxiety, or feeling like you're not enough. As you are guided through the five-step method in the following pages, you can accumulate what you've learned in this book to begin your journey to emotional transformation in your own unique and personal way.

Connect with a Certified FreedomPOINT Practitioner

If you're ready to experience personal transformation with myself or a Certified FreedomPOINT Practitioner, visit https://www. successmatrix.com/book-me/ to schedule a call.

STEP 1: PREPARE

As you begin your self-guided FreedomPOINT journey, remember that the purpose isn't to spiral into the past to rehash all the details of every scene in your Past ME movie. The first step is to simply contemplate what your "apple pie" stories are and prepare yourself for a successful session.

Begin by getting clear on your intentions and centering and grounding yourself, creating a calm, quiet, environment that's free of distractions. Remember that it's natural for your thoughts to wander; this is simply the silent chatter you'll need to quiet before starting the process. When your mind is fully present, you will experience a gap that is created in the mental thought process which causes the silent chatter of the mind to dissipate, then invites in stillness and peace to take its place. By quieting your mind and becoming more present through slow, deep breathing, prayer, and meditation, you will feel more alive, alert, and relaxed.

You can use the acronym FACE that you read about in Part II to help you prepare: Focus, Affirm, Center, Engage.

Focus

Close your eyes, relax your body, and imagine any distractions disappearing. You can direct your focus by repeating the statement "I am here now; I am ready to serve."

Affirm

Set your intention to serve only the highest good and release any
expectations you might have about the outcome of your session.

Center

Centering means creating alignment and awareness of your Emotional
Center (your heart), your Physical Center (your gut), your Mental Center
(your thinking mind), and your Spiritual Center (your intuition). You
can do this by doing a short meditation, taking some cleansing breaths
into your heart space, or recite a brief mantra or prayer.

Engage

Engage and expand your sensory acuity, which is simply your level
of paying attention. With heightened acuity, you will "hear" the
information the subconscious is presenting, as well as notice certain
clues through your body language, facial expressions, emotional
reactions, tears, sounds, and postures. You may also receive messages, or
"communication downloads" that come through your intuition. Invite
your senses to wake up, pay attention, and make astute observations.

Journal

PREPARE

- ❦ Journal about what you did to prepare.
- ❦ What did you notice through your FACE: Focus, Affirming, Centering, and Engaging?

....

....

....

....

....

....

....

....

....

....

....

....

....

....

....

....

....

....

....

....

....

STEP 2: OBSERVE

Now that you've identified your "apple pie" stories, it's time to observe *how those stories make you feel.* This is the point the stories begin to reveal their value.

Building self-awareness of your Current ME is the beginning to understanding the emotion patterns that have created your inner reality and what information they want to share with you. The more you practice listening to and paying particular attention to the undermining language patterns of others, the more naturally and frequently you'll tune into your own self-talk, repetitive questions, and limiting beliefs.

Journal

OBSERVE

- Journal about your self-talk, the emotions that are attached (how your self-talk makes you feel), and how you'd like to feel differently.

As you Observe, consider the following:

~ What words or metaphors are used in your self-talk that sound limiting? (Your self-talk might sound like, "My career is a total flop" or "I feel like I'm walking on thin ice.")

~ What are the feelings or emotions that are associated with your self-talk? Which ones are you focused on the most?

~ What questions do you ask yourself perpetually? (You might hear questions like, "What's wrong with me?" or "Why do I keep screwing this up?")

~ Which areas of your life feel the most stressful or difficult to navigate?

~ How could feeling differently change your life?

STEP 3: INQUIRE

Now it's time to do some self-inquiry to pinpoint where the emotions and feelings are showing up in your body. Inquiring means you must be able to sit with the emotions and ask the question, "Where is this emotion presenting in my body?" Be prepared that they may not show up for you immediately. You may go about doing your work, or washing the dishes, and suddenly, there it is!

POINTer

Controlling your breathing and noticing the movement of your body helps you relax and increases your overall awareness. The more you notice, the more aware you become, and the more aware you become, the more you notice.

Journal

INQUIRE

🦋 Journal about the information that shows up inside or outside the body.

Sit up straight with your feet on the floor and take some slow breaths in, then slowly exhale. Gently close your eyes and take a few more slow, deep breaths inhaling through the nose, and exhaling slowly and gently through the mouth. Continue to focus on your breath, then bring your attention to the movement of your body that accompanies the inhale and exhale, such as your belly expanding and rib cage opening on the inhale. Notice how your lungs expand, your chest lifts, and your shoulders shift slightly. As you exhale, notice how your belly contracts, your chest closes in, your lungs empty, and your shoulders drop. With each slow breath, you will find a deeper connection with your physical body, as well as with the information field outside of your body. Continue breathing and imagine you're breathing directly into your heart. Very quickly, you will begin to notice your heartbeat, perhaps through feeling a pulse or even hearing it beat.

Once you recognize where you feel something, whether inside or outside the body, you will further the inquiry with a few essential questions. As you journal, capture the answers that come quickly. Trust your intuitive/gut responses. When you think too much about the answers, you will only get the conclusions of the conscious mind.

As you Inquire, ask the following key questions:

~ "How long have you been here in service to me?"

~ "What job did you come to do?"

~ "What has been the upside to your service? What gifts, strengths, character qualities have you helped to develop?"

~ "What, if anything, has been the downside of your service and/ or strategy?

~ "Is that what you intended for me?"

~ "What do you really want for me?"

STEP 4: NEGOTIATE

You know your PAST ME stories, how they make you feel, and where they're showing up in your body. Now that you've determined the upside (the benefits of the emotions which have presented) you understand how your patterns worked to serve you throughout your life. And the downside was revealed so the subconscious can loosen its grip to release or modify the old pattern and give way to something new and more empowering.

POINTer

When is it time for a pattern to transform? The answer is, whenever there are more adverse consequences (downside) to running the pattern than there is upside. Journaling about the downside, or consequences of your current emotion patterns, enables you to dig deep and go beyond your conscious filters to identify what things are no longer serving your highest good.

It's time to negotiate a new program/pattern of belief, emotion, behavior, or perspective because the subconscious is now fully aware of the UNINTENDED DOWNSIDE of the current program.

Journal

NEGOTIATE

🦋 Journal about your emotion pattern strategies.

What emotional reactions are you having to the current strategies? What strategies are no longer tolerable and must change? (The downside might sound like, "I work him into a frenzy and stress him out" or "He gets so nervous, he can't sleep, loses his appetite, and gets short-tempered with others.")

Journaling about the upside of your emotion patterns helps you get clear on how they have served and benefited you. (The upside might sound like, "She is always prepared," "I help her stay organized," or "She works really hard to reach her goals, and we've gotten very good results; she just got promoted!")

As you Negotiate, ask the following key questions:

~ "Have you fulfilled your original intention?"

(If the answer is "Yes," ask):

~ "Is it Ok for you to go now?"

(If the answer is "No," ask):

~ "What do you need to change or add in order to fulfill the original intention and eliminate the downside?"

(e.g.: add confidence and self-trust and let go of the need for perfection)

....

....

....

STEP 5: TRANSFORM

You achieve transformation when your subconscious has communicated what your emotion patterns really want for you. Those patterns need to release or transform on some level. Adding new beliefs to an old operating system would only cause more inner turmoil because the conflict is still there under the surface. The butterfly of your Ideal ME can only emerge when the emotional inner conflict has been resolved through negotiation.

POINTer

To achieve transformation, you will discover a readiness within yourself— in every cell of your body—of what needs to change; then be open as to "how" it needs to change. Remember the three options for negotiating with your patterns: Delete them, install an upgrade, or install a new program.

In this step, you will release, upgrade, or draw in or upon new resources. This is a meditative visualization process, so as your subconscious chooses an option to transform the pattern, you'll want to visualize its release, intake, or merger of new patterns and resources. As you visualize the transformation of the pattern, it's important to pay close attention to the physical shifts that occur in your body. You might feel a lightheartedness, tingling, buzzing, or a wave of energy moving through you.

Journal

TRANSFORM

🦋 Journal about the options your emotion pattern(s) chose to transform and what feels different now. (Refer back to Part II, Step 5 to review information on the three options: Delete, Install an Upgrade, and Install a New Program.)

EXPANSION OPTION

If the pattern wishes to expand, ask the following question:

~ "Does the pattern wish to be stronger, bigger, or more intense?" (If "Yes," you can now amplify and expand its presence.)

Take another slow deep breath, and as you exhale, set the intention to expand the new information throughout the body. And with the next breath and intention, infuse it into every cell of the body.

POINTer

You can continue to amplify, magnify, and intensify as much as you want.

....

....

....

....

....

....

....

....

EPILOGUE

EPILOGUE

I BEGAN WRITING THIS book nearly ten years ago. I'm pretty sure God/ Source knew I wasn't ready, and even more significantly, God knew the work wasn't ready to be shared. There would be more insights to come, more clarity around how to teach this method of transformation, and yet another teacher I would encounter.

The teacher who was meant to come into my life was Mother Ayahuasca, the ancient plant wisdom from indigenous Amazonian cultures. I had no idea the influence this powerful plant medicine was going to have on my life and my work.

My quest began because of a comment I received from a client. After a mind-blowing, "other-worldly" session with Rolf, he said to me, "I tell all my friends about your work and describe you as the 'human ayahuasca.'" At that time, I didn't know what ayahuasca was, and having never experienced plant medicine of any kind, his comment really piqued my interest. I was curious what this comparison really meant.

A few years later, some friends who were traveling to Peru for a plant medicine retreat notified me that a space had opened in their group. When the invitation was extended to join them, it was clear to me: "I must be ready now."

In my first ayahuasca journey, I was "shown" the purpose of my work. My subconscious mind outlined how FreedomPOINT is designed to offer "safe passage home," home to the pure and powerful essence of who we really are. Ayahuasca "explained" we are all being called home to our Divine Nature. Labels, judgments, rules, and expectations from others have taken us away from the truth that we are all loved and worthy of receiving love. We are deserving of and have infinite access to every abundance of the Universe; no one is denied access for any reason.

The similarity between an ayahuasca journey and a FreedomPOINT session is found in the way it allows us to connect deeply with our physical body, shift our brain wave frequency, and tap into our subconscious/superconscious mind. It encourages the conscious mind to take a step back and "take notes" as the subconscious mind reveals its indescribable, omniscient genius. Please understand I have no intention to diminish the power of the conscious mind. It is brilliant in its function, working inextricably with the senses—the tangible environment to help us make sense of things and take effective action to secure the results we want. The subconscious receives millions of bits of information that are not visible, audible, or tangible to the senses, and yet it's able to filter all this information, providing guidance to ensure our safety, survival, and ability to thrive.

In the book, *Stealing Fire*, the authors describe multiple ways we can "tap into the zone." Drugs, health regimens, athlete's/runner's high and various spiritual practices like meditation, prayer, fasting, and psychedelics help us access a place of expanded abilities and flow. We pursue these experiences because something within us knows we are capable of more, and we are being called to express this greater capacity and potential.

On my first plant medicine retreat at Rythmia Life Advancement Center in Costa Rica, I received a direct message through Mother Ayahuasca:

"No noise, no drama, no fanfare required, be still and be transformed."

During my ayahuasca journey on my second trip to Rythmia, the message was:

*"Call together legions of the Noble Heart to help uplift human consciousness and restore compassion for all of life." I was told the Noble Heart is no ordinary heart. It is not selfish or selfless; it does not sacrifice or martyr. **"It has the power to put the needs of others ahead of itself."***

Because you are reading this book and have made it to this passage, I believe you are one of the Noble Hearts who is here to make an important difference in the world. Thank you for keeping your appointment.

If you choose to go deeper into this work and intend to develop mastery in creating transformation for yourself and others, please reach out to me at support@freedompointcoaching.com.

Thank you for inviting me to be a part of your journey as you embark on your "safe passage home."

In awe and wonder,

Deb

RESOURCES

Download Deb's FREE eBook *Stop That, Start This*

Stop That, Start This will teach you how to stop wasting time, losing momentum, and failing to execute so you can confidently move forward in your personal power, trusting yourself to do the important things at the right time, while staying on track with your ultimate goals. Visit https://www.successmatrix.com.

Connect with a Certified FreedomPOINT Practitioner

If you're ready to experience personal transformation with myself or a Certified FreedomPOINT Practitioner, visit https://www.successmatrix.com/book-me/ to schedule a call.

Book Me for Your Company

If you are a business leader who's ready to experience next-level results, learn more about how FreedomPOINT can help your company at https://www.successmatrix.com/book-deb-for-your-corporation/

Book Me for Individual or Group Coaching

If you are a committed entrepreneur who's ready to tap into your ultimate success genius, learn more about my tailored business coaching programs at https://www.successmatrix.com/business-coaching-programs/.

Become a Certified FreedomPOINT Practitioner

If you are interested in becoming a Certified FreedomPOINT Practitioner, visit https://www.successmatrix.com/freedompoint-certification/

ABOUT DEBORAH A. BATTERSBY

Deborah Battersby is a recognized pioneer in the fields of both emotional and behavioral transformation. Her expertise centers around peak performance and unlocking greater potential. She is a business success coach, inspirational speaker, author, and founder of Success Matrix Inc. For more than two decades, Deb has helped thousands of people gain greater personal power and life transformation through her innovative, leading-edge FreedomPOINT method. Deb and her Success Matrix team help their clients tap into the unstoppable power within themselves and close the gap between where they are and where they want to be and can be.

Deb is a compassionate rebel who dares to do things differently to get unprecedented results. An award-winning sales leader and acclaimed coach and trainer in Business and Personal Leadership, Deb has been blazing trails throughout her career. Her ability to bring out the best in all those she serves has attracted a global clientele across diverse industries. Her transformational coaching methods are engaged by entrepreneurs, business leaders, and top professionals, and her FreedomPOINT method (FPM) Certification is a sought-after credential for elite coaches around the world. She is a teacher, a guide, and, in her own words, a perpetual student. Deb holds Master Practitioner Certifications in the fields of neurolinguistics, neuro-associative conditioning, hypnotherapy, neuro-strategy, Emotional Freedom Technique, (EFT) as well as the healing modalities of Reiki and Deeksha. She is also distinguished as an elite Master Trainer with Robbins Research International.

Connect with Deb at:

https://www.successmatrix.com/

https://www.freedompointcoaching.com

Made in the USA
Columbia, SC
18 June 2022

61861312R00109